Diagnosing and Changing
Organizational Culture

WITHDRAWN

NW08000055 MANA

KU-790-543

N 0145544 3

Kim S. Cameron
Robert E. Quinn

NEWMAN UNIVERSITY
COLLEGE
BARTLEY GREEN
BIRMINGHAM B32 3NT

CLASS 658.406
BARCODE 0145443
AUTHOR CAM

Diagnosing and Changing Organizational Culture

**Based on the Competing
Values Framework**

REVISED EDITION

The Jossey-Bass
Business & Management Series

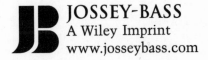

JOSSEY-BASS
A Wiley Imprint
www.josseybass.com

Copyright © 2006 by John Wiley & Sons, Inc. All rights reserved.

Published by Jossey-Bass
A Wiley Imprint
989 Market Street, San Francisco, CA 94103-1741   www.josseybass.com

No part of this publication may be reproduced, stored in a retrieval system, or transmitted in any form or by any means, electronic, mechanical, photocopying, recording, scanning, or otherwise, except as permitted under Section 107 or 108 of the 1976 United States Copyright Act, without either the prior written permission of the publisher, or authorization through payment of the appropriate per-copy fee to the Copyright Clearance Center, Inc., 222 Rosewood Drive, Danvers, MA 01923, 978-750-8400, fax 978-646-8600, or on the Web at www.copyright.com. Requests to the publisher for permission should be addressed to the Permissions Department, John Wiley & Sons, Inc., 111 River Street, Hoboken, NJ 07030, 201-748-6011, fax 201-748-6008, or online at www.wiley.com/go/permissions.

Limit of Liability/Disclaimer of Warranty: While the publisher and author have used their best efforts in preparing this book, they make no representations or warranties with respect to the accuracy or completeness of the contents of this book and specifically disclaim any implied warranties of merchantability or fitness for a particular purpose. No warranty may be created or extended by sales representatives or written sales materials. The advice and strategies contained herein may not be suitable for your situation. You should consult with a professional where appropriate. Neither the publisher nor author shall be liable for any loss of profit or any other commercial damages, including but not limited to special, incidental, consequential, or other damages.

Jossey-Bass books and products are available through most bookstores. To contact Jossey-Bass directly call our Customer Care Department within the U.S. at 800-956-7739, outside the U.S. at 317-572-3986, or fax 317-572-4002.

Jossey-Bass also publishes its books in a variety of electronic formats. Some content that appears in print may not be available in electronic books.

First edition was published under same title by Addison-Wesley in 1999.

Library of Congress Cataloging-in-Publication Data

Cameron, Kim S.
  Diagnosing and changing organizational culture : based on the competing values framework / Kim S. Cameron, Robert E. Quinn.—Revised ed.
      p. cm.—(The Jossey-Bass business & management series)
  Includes bibliographical references and index.
  ISBN-13 978-0-7879-8283-6 (alk. paper)
  ISBN-10 0-7879-8283-0 (alk. paper)
  1. Organizational change. 2. Corporate culture. I. Quinn, Robert E. II. Title. III. Series.
  HD58.8.C32 2006
  658.4'06—dc22

                                                                    2005023398

Printed in the United States of America
REVISED EDITION
PB Printing   10 9 8 7 6 5 4

Contents

Preface

This book was written to help you diagnose and initiate change in organizational culture, whether you are a manager, teacher, consultant, or change agent. We were motivated to write this book because of our own observation that organizations often fail in their change and improvement efforts because of their inability to bring about culture change. We were also motivated because of our conviction that the Competing Values Framework can be effectively applied to several important aspects of organizational and personal performance. We know of consulting firms in several countries that have adopted the framework as a key part of their services. And we know of business, government, and educational organizations that have dramatically improved their performance as a result of applying the processes and approaches explained in the book, as well as individual managers who have become more effective by personalizing the principles we discuss. Of course, we don't claim to have found a silver bullet or a panacea for all organizational and managerial problems. Rather, we have written the book to share a set of tools and procedures that our own empirical research and consulting experiences have found to be useful in assisting with cultural and personal change in organizations.

This book will be most useful to (1) consultants and change agents charged with helping organizations and managers implement change and with making sense of their own culture; (2) teachers interested in helping students understand organizational culture, the change process, and the power of theoretical frameworks in guiding change efforts; and (3) managers who are interested in identifying ways to effectively lead a culture change effort while finding ways to match their personal style and capabilities with the demands of the organization's future environment. This book, therefore, may be appropriate for the college classroom, the training and development center, the executive's bookshelf, or the conference table around which employees meet to participate in the culture change process.

This book offers you three contributions: (1) validated instruments for diagnosing organizational culture and management competency, (2) a theoretical framework for understanding organizational culture, and (3) a systematic strategy for changing organizational culture and personal behavior. It is intended to be a *workbook* in the sense that you can complete the instruments and plot your own culture profile in the book itself, and you can also use it as a resource for leading a culture change process. The management competency assessment instrument also helps facilitate personal change in support of the desired culture change. The book can also serve as an *information source* for explaining a robust framework of culture types. This framework has proved to be very useful to a variety of companies in clarifying the culture change process as well as instigating significant managerial leadership improvement.

In Chapter One, we discuss the importance of understanding organizational culture and its central place in facilitating or inhibiting organizational improvement efforts. We illustrate how culture change can foster dramatic improvement in organizational effectiveness or else how it can be the major obstacle that keeps organizations from fulfilling their objectives.

In Chapter Two, we provide the instrument for diagnosing organizational culture and instructions for how to complete and score it. This instrument—the Organizational Culture Assessment Instrument (OCAI)—produces an overall organizational culture profile. Six dimensions of organizational culture are assessed. The six dimensions are based on a theoretical framework of how organizations work and the kinds of values on which their cultures are founded. The OCAI identifies what the current organizational culture is like, as well as what the organization's preferred or future culture should be like.

Chapter Three provides a more thorough explanation of the theoretical framework on which the OCAI is based. This framework—the Competing Values Framework—explains the underlying value orientations that characterize organizations. These value orientations are usually competing or contradictory to one another. The chapter explains how these values, and the organizational cultures that emerge from them, change over time and how the framework is applicable for making sense of a variety of organizational phenomena, including structure, quality, leadership, and management skills.

Chapter Four contains a step-by-step process for producing an organizational culture profile, identifying the ways in which the organization's culture should change, and formulating a strategy for accomplishing that change. Information about the cultures of almost one thousand organizations is provided for comparison purposes.

Chapter Five provides a six-step methodology for guiding a culture change strategy. Also presented are examples of how several different organizations used the OCAI to diagnose their current and preferred organizational cultures. We illustrate how the organizations designed a strategy to change their current culture to better match their preferred culture. These examples and the methodology provide systematic guidelines to managers and change agents who are charged with changing their own organization's culture.

Chapter Six focuses on the personal change needed to support and facilitate culture change. It explains critical management competencies that are typical of effective managers, and it provides a methodology for helping managers develop a personal improvement agenda. Included is a diagnostic instrument that has been used with managers in more than a thousand organizations worldwide. Use of the diagnostic instrument is an important element in aligning managerial competencies with desired culture change.

Chapter Seven summarizes the key points in the book and provides a condensed summary formula to guide culture change efforts.

We provide five appendixes. Appendix A contains a more rigorous and scientifically based discussion of the OCAI and the Competing Values Framework. Its intent is to provide researchers and organizational scholars with the evidence they may require in order to use this instrument to study organizational cultures and culture change. Evidence for the validity and reliability of the OCAI is provided, as well as a discussion of cultural definitions and the powerful impact of cultural change on effectiveness. This material may be of greater interest to researchers and organizational scholars than to managers and change agents.

Appendix B provides an instrument that helps managers identify the key competencies they will need to develop or improve in order to foster organizational culture change. A discussion of the instrument's validity and usefulness precedes the presentation of the questions themselves. The instrument is the Management Skills Assessment Instrument (MSAI). Information is provided for obtaining scoring and feedback reports for managers who are involved in the culture change effort as part of the strategy to align management competencies with the organizational culture change initiative.

Appendix C provides suggestions for initiating culture change in each of four types of cultures. These suggestions are provided merely as thought starters and idea generators when extra help is needed. They have come from managers and change agents who have engaged in the culture change process described in this book.

Appendix D provides lists of suggestions for improving management skills and competencies associated with the MSAI. These suggestions were generated by managers who have successfully implemented personal change efforts in improving their own managerial competencies.

Appendix E contains some extra plotting forms and profile forms to be used as part of the culture change initiative.

September 2005
Ann Arbor, Michigan

Kim S. Cameron
Robert E. Quinn

Acknowledgments

We have been educated and informed by many colleagues in our work on organizational culture over the years. In particular, Jeff De Graff, Robert Hooijberg, and Frank Petrock have helped us think through the culture change methodology. Several of our colleagues have conducted insightful and informative research on our framework, including Wayne Brockbank, Lee Collett, Dan Denison, Susan Faerman, Sarah Freeman, Jack Krackower, Michael McGrath, Carlos Mora, John Rohrbaugh, Gretchen Spreitzer, Michael Thompson, David Ulrich, Arthur Yeung, and Ray Zammuto. Outstanding insights and suggestions were provided on the book manuscript by Dick Beckhard, Ed Schein, and Jon Van Maanen, and helpful reviews by Peter Frost, Tom Gregoire, and Deone Zell. Particular thanks are due to our editor, Kathe Sweeney at Jossey-Bass, for her continued support and friendship, and to a very competent support team led by Jessie Mandle at Jossey-Bass. Of course, even though we would like to blame these folks for any mistakes, oversights, or wrong-headed thinking that might remain in the manuscript, we accept responsibility for it. They have done their best with us.

Most important, we want to acknowledge and thank our sweethearts, Melinda and Delsa, and our children, Katrina Cameron Powley, Tiara Cameron Wartes, Asher Cameron, Cheyenne Cameron Robertson, Brittany Cameron Corbett, Austin Cameron, and Cam Cameron, as well as Shauri Quinn, Ryan Quinn, Shawn Quinn, Kristin Quinn Ellis, Travis Quinn, and Garrett Quinn. Their love of one another and of us has created a culture that we never want to change.

K.S.C.
R.E.Q.

The Authors

Kim S. Cameron is professor of management and organization at the University of Michigan Business School and professor of higher education in the School of Education at the University of Michigan. He has served as dean and Albert J. Weatherhead Professor of Management in the Weatherhead School of Management at Case Western Reserve University, as associate dean and Ford Motor Co./Richard E. Cook Professor in the Marriott School of Management at Brigham Young University, and as a department chair and director of several executive education programs at the University of Michigan. He also served on the faculties of the University of Wisconsin-Madison and Ricks College. He organized and directed the Organizational Studies Division of the National Center for Higher Education Management Systems in Boulder, Colorado.

Cameron's past research on organizational virtuousness, downsizing, effectiveness, culture, and the development of leadership excellence has been published in more than eighty articles and nine books: *Coffin Nails and Corporate Strategies* (Prentice Hall, 1982), *Developing Management Skills* (Prentice Hall, 6th ed., 2005), *Diagnosing and Changing Organizational Culture* (Addison-Wesley, 1999), *Organizational Decline* (Ballinger, 1988), *Leading with Values* (Cambridge, 2006), *Organizational Effectiveness* (Academic Press, 1983), *Paradox and Transformation* (Ballinger, 1988), *Positive Organizational Scholarship* (Berrett-Koehler, 2003), and *The Competing Values Framework* (Elgar, 2006). His current research is on the positive dynamics in organizations that lead to spectacular performance. Specifically, he has been funded to study virtuousness in organizations and its relationship to performance.

Cameron received his bachelor of science and master of science degrees from Brigham Young University and his master of arts and doctoral degrees from Yale University. He served on the National Research Council, was president of Bay Asset Funding Corporation, and was a Fulbright Distinguished Scholar. He is a graduate of Leadership Cleveland Class of 2000 and a recipient of the Organizational Behavior Teaching Society's Outstanding Educator award. He currently consults with a variety of business, government, and educational organizations in North America, South America, Asia, Europe, and Africa.

He is married to the former Melinda Cummings and has seven children.

Robert E. Quinn holds the Margaret Elliot Tracey Collegiate Professorship at the University of Michigan and serves on the organization and management faculty at the University of Michigan Business School. He is one of the cofounders of the Center for Positive Organizational Scholarship. Quinn's research and teaching interests focus on organizational change and effectiveness. He has published fourteen books on these subjects.

He is particularly known for his work on the Competing Values Framework, recognized as one of the forty most important models in the history of business. Using his approach, researchers have generated numerous books and articles to clarify complex dynamics surrounding topics in many disciplines. Practitioners across all sectors, in many organizations, have used his work to transform both culture and practice. Furthermore, thousands of managers have trained in his methods at the University of Michigan and through the use of his textbooks. He has personally assisted numerous large organizations in the process of change.

His B.S. and M.S. degrees were obtained from Brigham Young University and his Ph.D. from the University of Cincinnati. He and his wife, Delsa, have six children, Shauri, Ryan, Shawn, Kristin, Travis, and Garrett.

In recent years, Quinn has completed a trilogy of books on personal and organizational transformation: the best seller *Deep Change: Discovering the Leader Within* (1996), *Change the World: How Ordinary People Can Accomplish Extraordinary Results* (2000), and *Building the Bridge as You Walk on It: A Guide to Change* (2004), all published by Jossey-Bass. At the Center for Positive Organizational Scholarship, he is currently working on questions concerning extraordinary performance.

1

AN INTRODUCTION TO CHANGING ORGANIZATIONAL CULTURE

No organization in the twenty-first century would boast about its constancy, sameness, or status quo compared to ten years ago. Stability is interpreted more often as stagnation than steadiness, and organizations that are not in the business of change and transition are generally viewed as recalcitrant. The frightening uncertainty that traditionally accompanied major organizational change has been superseded by the frightening uncertainty now associated with staying the same.

The father of modern management, Peter Drucker, concluded that "We are in one of those great historical periods that occur every 200 or 300 years when people don't understand the world anymore, and the past is not sufficient to explain the future" (quoted in Childress and Senn, 1995, p. 3) Unremitting, unpredictable, and sometimes alarming change makes it difficult for any organization or manager to stay current, to accurately predict the future, and to maintain constancy of direction. The failure rate of most planned organizational change initiatives is dramatic. It is well known, for example, that as many as three-quarters of reengineering, total quality management (TQM), strategic planning, and downsizing efforts have failed entirely or have created problems serious enough that the survival of the organization was threatened (Cameron, 1997). What is most interesting about these failures, however, is the reported reasons for their lack of success. Several studies reported that the most frequently cited reason given for failure was a neglect of the organization's culture. In other words, failure to change the organization's culture doomed the other kinds of organizational

1

changes that were initiated (Caldwell, 1994; CSC Index, 1994; Gross, Pascale, and Athos, 1993; Kotter and Heskett, 1992).

Our purpose in this book is not to offer one more panacea for coping with our turbulent times or to introduce another management fad. We agree with Tom Peters that in the current high-velocity environment, "if you're not confused, you're not paying attention." Confusion abounds, as do prescriptions and proposed panaceas. Instead, our intent in this book is both more modest and, we believe, potentially more helpful. The book provides a framework, a sensemaking tool, a set of systematic steps, and a methodology for helping managers and their organizations adapt to the demands of the environment. It focuses less on the right answers than it does on the methods and mechanisms available to help managers change the most fundamental elements of their organizations. It provides a way for managers almost anywhere in the hierarchy of an organization, to guide the change process at the most basic level—the cultural level. It provides a systematic strategy for internal or external change agents to facilitate fundamental change that can then support and supplement other kinds of change initiatives.

The Need to Manage Organizational Culture

Most of the scholarly literature argues that successful companies—those with sustained profitability and above-normal financial returns—are characterized by certain well-defined conditions (originally identified by Porter, 1980). Six such conditions are believed to be crucial. The first is the presence of high barriers to entry. When other organizations face difficult obstacles to engaging in the same business as your organization—for example, high costs, special technology, or proprietary knowledge—few, if any, competitors will exist. Fewer competitors means more revenues for your firm. A second condition is nonsubstitutable products. When other organizations cannot duplicate your firm's product or service and no alternatives exist—for example, you are the sole supplier of a product or service—it stands to reason that revenues are likely to be higher. Third, a large market share enhances success by allowing your firm to capitalize on economies of scale and efficiencies. The biggest player in a market can negotiate concessions, sell at a discount, vertically integrate, or even purchase smaller competitors, thereby generating more revenues. A fourth condition is low levels of bargaining power for buyers. For example, if purchasers of your firm's products become dependent on your company because they have no alternative sources, higher revenues are an obvious result. Fifth, suppliers have low levels of bargaining power. When suppliers, like customers, become dependent on your company because they have no alternative, you will have higher levels of financial returns. They must sell to you, making it possible for your firm to negotiate favorable prices and time schedules, higher levels of quality, or more proprietary features. The sixth and final condition is rivalry among competitors. Rivalry helps deflect attention away from head-to-head competition with your company. Competitors struggle against one another instead of targeting your firm as the central focus of attack. Equally important, stiff competition is likely to raise the standards of performance in the entire industry. Incentives to improve are a product of rigorous competition (see Porter, 1980).

Unquestionably, these are desirable features that clearly should enhance financial success. They seem pretty much common sense. However, what is remarkable is that the most successful U.S. firms in the past twenty years have had none of these competitive advantages. The top five performers in the past two decades—those who have literally blown away the competition in financial returns—have not been the recipients of any of the so-called prerequisites for success. These highly successful firms are Southwest Airlines (21,775% return), Wal-Mart (19,807% return), Tyson Foods (18,118% return), Circuit City (16,410% return), and Plenum Publishing (15,689% return) (Compustat Data Services, 2005).

Think of it. If you were going to start a business and wanted to make a killing, the markets you will most likely avoid are airlines, discount retailing, food distribution, consumer electronic sales, and publishing. The list of industries represented by these five highly successful firms looks like an impending disaster for new entrants—massive competition, horrendous losses, widespread bankruptcy, virtually no barriers to entry, little unique technology, and many substitute products and services. None of these firms entered the industry with a leadership position in market share. Yet these five firms have outperformed all rivals, even with no special competitive advantages.

What differentiates these extraordinarily successful firms from others? How have they been able to make it when others have failed? How did Wal-Mart take on Sears and Kmart—the two largest retailers in the world—and, figuratively speaking, eat their lunch? While Wal-Mart prospered, its largest rivals were forced to sell off divisions, replace CEOs (more than once), downsize dramatically, and close stores wholesale. How did Southwest Airlines thrive when several of its competitors went belly-up (remember Eastern, Pan Am, Texas Air, PeopleExpress)? How did Circuit City, Tyson Foods, and Plenum Publishing succeed when their competitors have gone out of business so rapidly that it's hard to keep up? The key ingredient in each case is something less tangible, less blatant, but more powerful than the market factors listed earlier. The major distinguishing feature in these companies, their most important competitive advantage, the most powerful factor they all highlight as a key ingredient in their success, is their organizational culture.

The sustained success of these firms has had less to do with market forces than with company values, less to do with competitive positioning than with personal beliefs, and less to do with resource advantages than with vision. In fact, it is difficult to name even a single highly successful company, one that is a recognized leader in its industry, that does not have a distinctive, readily identifiable organizational culture. Name the most successful firms you know today, from large behemoths like Coca-Cola, Disney, General Electric, Intel, McDonald's, Microsoft, Rubbermaid, Sony, and Toyota to small entrepreneurial start-ups. Virtually every leading firm you can name, small or large, has developed a distinctive culture that is clearly identifiable by its employees. This culture is sometimes created by the initial founder of the firm (such as Walt Disney). Sometimes it emerges over time as an organization encounters and overcomes challenges and obstacles in its environment (as at Coca-Cola). Sometimes it is developed consciously by management teams who decide to improve their company's performance in systematic ways (as General Electric did). Simply stated, successful companies have developed something special that supersedes corporate strategy, market presence, and technological advantages. Although strategy, market presence, and technology are clearly important, highly successful firms have capitalized on the power that resides in developing and managing a unique corporate culture. This power abides in the ability of a strong, unique culture to reduce collective uncertainties (that is, facilitate a common interpretation system for members), create social order (make clear to members what is expected), create continuity (perpetuate key values and norms across generations of members), create a collective identity and commitment (bind members together), and elucidate a vision of the future (energize forward movement) (see Trice and Beyer, 1993).

Most organizational scholars and observers now recognize that organizational culture has a powerful effect on the performance and long-term effectiveness of organizations. Empirical research has produced an impressive array of findings demonstrating the importance of culture to enhancing organizational performance (for reviews, see Cameron and Ettington, 1988; Denison, 1990; and Trice and Beyer, 1993).

Kotter and Heskett (1992) interviewed seventy-five highly regarded financial analysts whose job is to closely follow certain industries and corporations. Each analyst compared the performance of twelve highly successful firms to ten lower-performing firms. Although analysts are stereotyped as focusing almost exclusively on hard data, only one of the seventy-five indicated that culture had little or no impact on firm performance. All acknowledged culture as a critical factor in long-term financial success. In Appendix A, we summarize several scientific studies that report a positive relationship between dimensions of organizational culture and organizational effectiveness. For those interested in empirical evidence that supports the assessment procedures and culture change methodology explained in this book, Appendix A will be a helpful review of the academic literature.

In addition to organization-level effects, the impact of organizational culture on individuals (employee morale, commitment, productivity, physical health, emotional well-being) is also well documented (for a review, see Kozlowski, Chao, Smith, and Hedlund, 1993). With health care costs still skyrocketing, burnout at an all-time high, erosion of employee loyalty to firms costing millions of dollars a year in replacement and retraining, organizational secrets lost due to sabotage and defections, and lawsuits and other forms of retribution by disaffected employees, the impact of an organization's underlying culture on individuals is also an important area of concern. Moreover, we will explain later in the book that culture change, at its root, is intimately tied to individual change. Unless managers are willing to commit to personal change, the organization's culture will remain recalcitrant.

Our main focus in this book is on helping managers, change agents, and scholars facilitate and manage organizational culture change. Our purpose is to help individuals adopt effective ways of diagnosing and changing culture in order to enhance organizational performance. We provide a framework as well as a methodology for implementing this change process, and we integrate a model of individual-level change as a way to foster cultural transformation and to align personal managerial behavior with the culture change. Since culture is such a crucial factor in the long-term effectiveness of organizations, it is imperative that the individuals charged with studying or managing organizational culture be able to measure key dimensions of culture, develop a strategy for changing it, and begin an implementation process. This book helps accomplish those aims.

We begin by discussing the critical need for culture change in most modern organizations. Frequent and chaotic vacillations in the external environment create the risk that the existing organizational culture will inhibit rather than contribute to future corporate success. We also briefly address the meaning of the term *organizational culture*. To understand how culture change can enhance organizational performance, it is important that we make clear what is and isn't culture. All this establishes a groundwork for introducing our framework of the core dimensions of organizational culture. Along with that framework, we introduce an instrument and a method for diagnosing and initiating cultural change, and we supplement that with a personal management competency assessment instrument and improvement tool that is congruent with the framework. We provide some examples of companies that have successfully implemented our methodology, and we provide some practical hints for how others might successfully implement culture change.

This book, in other words, serves both as a workbook and as a source guide. It is a workbook in the sense that it assists managers and change agents to work through a systematic culture diagnosis and change effort. It helps profile the current state of organizational culture and a preferred culture for the future, and it outlines a process for moving from the current to the preferred state. It also links a personal change methodology to an organizational change methodology.

The book serves as a source guide in the sense that it helps explain the core dimensions of culture and presents a theoretical framework for understanding culture forms. That is, the book explains what to look for when initiating culture change and the ways in which individual change and organizational change are linked. For individuals interested in examining the validity of this approach to culture change, a summary of scientific evidence is presented in Appendix One.

The Need for Culture Change

As mentioned earlier, change in organizations is pervasive because of the degree and rapidity of change in the external environment. The conditions in which organizations operate demand a response without which organizational demise is a frequent result. Of the largest one hundred companies at the beginning of the 1900s, for example, only sixteen are still in existence. Of the firms on *Fortune* magazine's first list of the five hundred biggest companies, only twenty-nine firms would still be included. During the past decade, 46 percent of the Fortune 500 dropped off the list.

Such dramatic change in organizational survival and effectiveness is understandable when considering the shift in the developed world from an industrial-age economy to an information-age economy. For the first time, beginning in the 1990s, companies spent more money on computing and communications gear than on industrial, mining, farm, and construction equipment combined. Whereas in the 1960s, approximately half of the workers in industrialized countries were involved in making tangible things, by the year 2000, no developed country had more than one-eighth of its workforce in the traditional roles of making and moving goods. This shift away from industrialization and toward information is also illustrated by the fact that more information was produced last year than was produced in the previous five thousand years. A weekday edition of the *New York Times* or the *International Herald Tribune* contains more information than the average person was likely to come across in a lifetime during the eighteenth century. The total amount of information available to the average person doubles every year.

The rate of technological change associated with this information explosion has created an environment intolerant of the status quo. Today's average wristwatch contains more computing power than existed in the entire world before 1960. The technology currently exists to put the equivalent of a full-size computer in a wristwatch or to inject the equivalent of a laptop computer into the bloodstream. The newest computers are relying on etchings onto molecules instead of silicone wafers. The mapping of the human genome is probably the greatest source for change, for not only can a banana now be changed into an agent to inoculate people against malaria, but new organ development and physiological regulations promise to dramatically alter people's lifestyles. Over a hundred animals have been patented to date, and four million new patent applications are filed each year related to bioengineering (Enriquez, 2000). Almost no one dares predict the changes that will occur in the next ten years. Moreover, not only is change ubiquitous and unpredictable, but almost everyone assumes that its velocity will increase exponentially (Cameron, 2003; Quinn, 2000). Such rapid and dramatic change implies that no organization can remain the same for long and survive. The current challenge, therefore, is not to determine whether to change but how to change to increase organizational effectiveness. The demise of some of the Fortune 500 companies undoubtedly resulted from slow, laggard, or wrongheaded change efforts.

For instance, the three most common organizational change initiatives implemented in the last two decades are TQM initiatives, downsizing initiatives, and reengineering initiatives (Cameron, 1997). Organizations that have implemented quality initiatives in order to enhance effectiveness, however, have by and large fallen short. Rath and Strong (a consulting firm) surveyed Fortune 500 companies and found that only 20 percent reported having achieved their quality objectives, and over 40 percent indicated that their quality initiatives were a complete flop. A study of thirty quality programs by McKinsey (another consulting firm) found that two-thirds had stalled, fallen short, or failed. And Ernst and Young's study of 584 companies in four industries (autos, banks, computers, and health care) in the United States, Japan, Germany, and Canada found that most firms had not successfully implemented their total quality practices. Most firms labeled TQM a failure and were actually cutting back their quality budgets (see Cameron, 1997, for details of various studies, including those mentioned here).

Similarly, nearly every organization of moderate size or larger has engaged in downsizing in the past decade. Downsizing has been another attempt to improve productivity, efficiency, competitiveness, and effectiveness. Unfortunately, two-thirds of companies that downsize end up doing it again a year later, and the stock prices of firms that downsized during the 1990s actually lagged the industry average a decade later. A survey of corporate executives in six industrialized countries found that less than half had achieved their cost-cutting goals and even fewer met operating objectives such as improved productivity. Another survey found that 74 percent of senior managers in downsized companies said that morale, trust, and productivity suffered after downsizing, and half of the 1,468 firms in still another survey indicated that productivity deteriorated after downsizing. Almost three-quarters of firms in another study were found to be worse off in the long term after downsizing than they were before. A majority of organizations that downsized in a fourth survey failed to achieve desired results, with only 9 percent reporting an improvement in quality. These outcomes led one editorialist to accuse organizations of "dumbsizing" instead of downsizing and another writer to conclude that "downsizing, as commonly practiced, is a dud" (see Cameron, 1997, for complete references).

A third common approach to enhancing organizational performance has been reengineering, the attempt to completely redesign the processes and procedures in an organization. Similar to TQM and downsizing initiatives, however, evidence suggests that this approach to change has also had a checkered success record. A survey was conducted of reengineering projects by the consulting firm that invented the reengineering change process (CSC Index, 1994). In all, 497 companies in the United States and another 1,245 companies in Europe were polled. The results showed that 69 percent of the firms in the United States and 75 percent of the firms in Europe had engaged in at least one reengineering project. Unfortunately, 85 percent of those firms reported little or no gain from their effort. Less than half, for example, achieved any change in market share, one of the primary goals. The authors concluded that reengineering was not enough to achieve desirable change. It had to be integrated with an overall approach to changing an organization's culture. In other words, the failure of reengineering (as well as TQM and downsizing) occurred in most cases because the culture of the organization remained the same. The procedure was treated as a technique or program of change, not as a fundamental shift in the organization's direction, values, and culture.

The point we are reiterating with these examples is that without another kind of fundamental change, namely, a change in organizational culture, there is little hope of enduring improvement in organizational performance. Although the tools and techniques may be present and the change strategy implemented with vigor, many efforts to improve organizational performance fail because the fundamental culture of the organization—values, ways of thinking, managerial styles, paradigms, approaches to problem solving—remains the same.

Extensive evidence of this fact has emerged from empirical studies conducted in more than one hundred organizations that had engaged in TQM and downsizing as strategies for enhancing effectiveness (Cameron, 1995, 1998; Cameron, Bright, and Caza, 2004; Cameron, Freeman, and Mishra, 1991). The results of those studies were unequivocal. The successful implementation of both TQM and downsizing programs, as well as the resulting effectiveness of the organizations' performance, depended on having the improvement strategies embedded in a culture change. When TQM and downsizing were implemented independent of a culture change, they were unsuccessful. When the culture of these organizations was an explicit target of change, so that the TQM or downsizing initiatives were embedded in an overall culture change effort, they were successful. Organizational effectiveness increased. Culture change was key.

This dependence of organizational improvement on culture change is due to the fact that when the values, orientations, definitions, and goals stay constant—even when procedures and strategies are altered—organizations return quickly to the status quo. The same is true for individuals. Personality types, personal styles, and behavioral habits rarely change significantly, despite programs to induce change such as diets, exercise regimens, or charm schools. Without an alternation of the fundamental goals, values, and expectations of organizations or individuals, change remains superficial and of short duration (see Quinn, 1996). Failed attempts to change, unfortunately, often produce cynicism, frustration, loss of trust, and deterioration in morale among organization members. As our research has shown, organizations may be worse off than if the change strategy had not been attempted in the first place. Modifying organizational culture, in other words, is a key to the successful implementation of major improvement strategies (TQM, downsizing, reengineering) as well as adaptation to the increasing turbulent environment faced by modern organizations.

The Power of Culture Change

Consider the well-known case of General Motors' auto assembly plant in Fremont, California. In the 1950s, General Motors had embarked on what was referred to as a "sunbelt strategy": plants were built in the southern and western states. Because these are all "right to work" states (with few unions), the United Auto Workers (UAW) viewed this as a union-avoidance move on the part of the company. But ultimately, not only were the new GM plants organized by the UAW, but they became among the most hostile, conflict-ridden plants in the entire corporation. Particularly troublesome was the plant in Fremont, California, where the Chevrolet Nova was assembled. It was a huge facility with several million square feet under one roof. By 1982, the plant was operating at a disastrously low level. Absenteeism averaged 20 percent per year, and approximately five thousand grievances were filed each year by employees at the plant—the same as the total number of workers. It also translates to about twenty-one formally filed grievances each working day! More than two thousand of those grievances remained unresolved. Three or four times each year, a wildcat strike would occur (people just walked off the job). Costs of assembling the car were 30 percent above those of its Japanese competitors, sales were trending downward, and ratings of both quality and productivity ranked the Fremont plant the worst in the company. Moreover, customer satisfaction with the Chevy Nova had hit rock bottom.

A variety of improvement programs had been tried—quality circles, employee relations initiatives, statistical process control, new incentive systems, tighter controls, downsizing, to name a few. Nothing worked. Quality, productivity, and satisfaction levels remained abysmal. Of course, it doesn't take a rocket scientist to figure out that the company could not afford to continue operating at that level of performance. The reputation of the entire corporation and all its divisions (Cadillac, Buick, Oldsmobile, Pontiac, Chevrolet, and GMC) was being negatively affected by the poor-quality product, the cost of simply keeping the plant running was overly burdensome, and management had nothing but grief from this group of employees. The decision was made to close the plant at the end of 1982.

Then GM did something interesting. The company approached its best competitor, Toyota, and offered to design and build a car together. GM was losing market share to Toyota, the Toyota production system was generally regarded as the best in the world at the time, and GM was having a difficult time trying to figure out how to fix its disastrous performance record, especially with the now-defunct Fremont plant. Toyota jumped at the chance. After all, GM was the world's largest company with the world's largest supplier and dealer networks, and it was a chance for Toyota to establish a firm footing on U.S. soil. GM offered to use the Fremont facility, but the plant was not to be remodeled. Old equipment had to be used. Toyota said, "Fine." GM indicated that because of the labor agreement, the joint venture couldn't hire just anyone. UAW workers had to be hired first, and they would come back on the basis of seniority. The oldest and most recalcitrant employees, the ones who had complained about management the longest, were given first crack at jobs. Toyota said, "Fine." Toyota had just one request, and that was to allow Toyota managers to run the place, not GM managers. GM said, "Fine." In late 1985, the plant was opened. The name was changed to NUMMI—New United Motors Manufacturing Incorporated. For the first two years, the Chevy Nova was produced; then it was phased out and replaced by the Geo Prism and the Toyota Corolla. Table 1.1 shows the performance data for the Fremont plant and the NUMMI plant after one year of operation, at the end of 1986.

Sales trends at the NUMMI plant were positive, quality and customer satisfaction were the highest in the company, the Toyota Corolla had fewer glitches than the comparable car produced in Japan, and productivity doubled the corporate average. Two decades later, the NUMMI plant continues to lead the company in most months in quality and productivity. Although more than twenty years old, this experiment still serves as an example to GM (and to other manufacturing businesses) of the dramatic improvement that is possible.

How did the turnaround occur? What accounts for the dramatic improvement in performance? Multiple factors were involved, of course, but the best explanation of the most important factor can be illustrated by an interview with one of the production employees at NUMMI. He had worked in the facility for more than twenty

Table 1.1 Comparison of GM's Fremont and NUMMI Plants

	1982 GM Fremont Plant	1986 GM NUMMI Plant
Employees	5,000	2,500
Absenteeism	20%	2%
Unresolved grievances	2,000	0
Total annual grievances	5,000	2
Wildcat strikes	3–4	0
Product	Chevrolet Nova	Chevrolet Nova 1988 Geo Prism Toyota Corolla
Assembly costs per car	30% over Japanese	Same as Japanese
Productivity	Worst in GM	Double GM average
Quality	Worst in GM	Best in GM

years. He was asked to describe the difference he experienced between the plant while it was managed by GM and the plant after the joint venture was formed. This UAW member said that prior to the joint venture, he would go home at night chuckling to himself about the things he had thought up during the day to mess up the system. He'd leave his sandwich behind the door panel of a car, for example. "Three months later, the customer would be driving down the road and wouldn't be able to figure out where that terrible smell was coming from. It would be my rotten sandwich in the door," he chuckled to himself. Or he would put loose screws in a compartment of the frame that was to be welded shut. People riding in the car would never be able to tell exactly where that rattle was coming from because it would reverberate throughout the entire car. "They'll never figure it out," he said.

"Now," he commented, "because the number of job classifications has been so dramatically reduced [from more than 150 to 6], we have all been allowed to have personal business cards and to make up our own titles. The title I put on my card is 'director of welding improvement.'" His job was to monitor certain robots that spot-welded parts of the frame together. "Now when I go to a San Francisco 49ers game or a Golden State Warriors game or a shopping mall, I look for Geo Prisms and Toyota Corollas in the parking lot. When I see one, I take out my business card and write on the back of it, 'I made your car. Any problems, call me.' I put it under the windshield wiper of the car. I do it because I feel personally responsible for those cars."

The difference between Fremont in 1982 and Fremont in 1992, at the time the interview was conducted, is a reflection of an organizational culture change. It was a gut-level, values-centered, in-the-bones change from viewing the world one way in 1982 to viewing it entirely differently a decade later. Employees had simply adopted a different way to think about the company and their role in it. Higher levels of productivity, quality, efficiency, and morale followed directly from this change in the firm's culture.

This is the kind of change that this book addresses. Unless it is integrated with other types of change initiatives—for example, TQM, downsizing, or reengineering—it is unlikely that the changes will be successful. The status quo will prevail. We repeat: without culture change, there is little hope for enduring improvement in organizational performance.

The Meaning of Organizational Culture

It was not until the beginning of the 1980s that organizational scholars began paying serious attention to the concept of culture (for example, Ouchi, 1981; Pascale and Athos, 1981; Peters and Waterman, 1982; Deal and Kennedy, 1982). This is one of the few areas, in fact, where organizational scholars led practicing managers in identifying a crucial factor affecting organizational performance. In most instances, practice has led research, and scholars have focused mainly on documenting, explaining, and building models of organizational phenomena that were already being tried by management. Organizational culture, however, has been an area in which conceptual work and scholarship have provided guidance for managers as they have searched for ways to improve their organizations' effectiveness.

The reason organizational culture was ignored as an important factor in accounting for organizational performance is that it encompasses the taken-for-granted values, underlying assumptions, expectations, collective memories, and definitions present in an organization. It represents "how things are around here." It reflects the prevailing ideology that people carry inside their heads. It conveys a sense of identity to employees, provides unwritten and often unspoken guidelines for how to get along in the organization, and it enhances the stability of the social system that they experience.[1] Unfortunately, people are unaware of their culture until it is challenged, until they experience a new culture, or until it is made overt and explicit through, for example, a framework or model. This is why culture was ignored for so long by managers and scholars. It is undetectable most of the time.

Of course, there are many kinds or levels of culture that affect individual and organizational behavior. At the broadest level, a global culture, such as a world religion's culture or the culture of the Far East would be the highest level. Researchers such as Hofstede (1980), Aiken and Bacharach (1979), and Trompenaars (1992) have reported marked differences among continents and countries based on certain key dimensions. For example, national differences exist among countries on the basis of universalism versus particularism, individualism versus collectivism, neutrality versus emotionality, specificity versus diffuseness, focus on achievement versus ascription, focus on past versus present versus future, and an internal focus versus an external focus (Trompenaars, 1992).

At a less general level are subgroups such as gender-based cultures (distinctive ways in which men and women view the world, as documented in Martin, 1990, or in Cox's 1991 work on differences between black and white cultures), occupational cultures (such as Van Maanen's 1975 studies of police culture), regional cultures (such as Blauner's 1964 work on regional and urban-rural cultures in the United States), and industry cultures (such as Gordon's 1991 work on competitiveness, historical development, core technology, and customer requirements that affect industry cultures). Each culture is generally reflected by unique language, symbols, rules, and ethnocentric feelings. Still less broad is the culture of a single organization, the level at which this book is aimed. An organization's culture is reflected by what is valued, the dominant leadership styles, the language and symbols, the procedures and routines, and the definitions of success that make an organization unique.

Inside an organization, subunits such as functional departments, product groups, hierarchical levels, or even teams may also reflect their own unique cultures. Difficulties in coordinating and integrating processes or organizational activities, for example, are often a result of culture clashes among different subunits. For instance, it is common in many organizations to hear of conflicts between marketing and manufacturing or of disparaging comments about the HR department or put-downs of the "white coats" in R&D. One reason is that each different unit often has developed its own perspective, its own set of values, its own culture. A variety of investigators have reported on the dysfunctions of subgroup culture clashes (Van Maanen and Barley, 1984, 1985; Jerimier, Slocum, Fry, and Gaines, 1991). It is easy to see how these cultural differences can fragment an organization and make high levels of effectiveness impossible to achieve. Emphasizing subunit cultural differences, in other words, can foster alienation and conflict.

On the other hand, it is important to keep in mind that each subunit in an organization also contains common elements typical of the entire organization. Similar to a hologram in which each unique element in the image contains the characteristics of the entire image in addition to its own identifying characteristics, subunit cultures also contain core elements of the entire organization's culture in addition to their own unique elements (Alpert and Whetten, 1985). There is always an underlying glue that binds the organization together (Schein, 1985; O'Reilly, Chatman, and Caldwell, 1991). In assessing an organization's culture, therefore, one can focus on the entire organization as the unit of analysis, or one can assess different subunit cultures, identify the common dominant attributes of the subunit cultures, and aggregate them. This combination can provide an approximation of the overall organizational culture.

In this book, we are interested primarily in helping managers identify ways in which their organization's culture can be diagnosed and changed. The relevant level of cultural analysis, therefore, is the level at which change efforts are directed. This may be at the overall organization level, or it may be at the level of a subunit supervised by a manager. The target is the level at which culture change is required for organizational performance to improve.

Caveats

We do not claim that our framework or our methodology represents the one best or the one right way to diagnose and change organizational culture. Doing so would be similar to claiming that one best way exists to design an organization, that one best leadership style exists, that one best method exists for measuring organizations, or that one best set of dimensions accounts for organizational success. None of these claims, of course, is reasonable. Other authors have proposed approaches to measuring organizational culture. Other frameworks have been proposed in the literature. A variety of underlying dimensions of culture have been put forward. Some authors have even denied that assessment and change of organizational culture are possible (Fitzgerald, 1988, is one). Although we review a sampling of alternative approaches in Chapter Three, our intent is not to provide an extensive review of the culture literature in this book. We have done so elsewhere (see Cameron, and Ettington, 1988; Beyer and Cameron, 1997). Instead, we are advocating here an approach that has several important advantages to managers and change agents interested in diagnosing and changing culture as well as to scholars interested in investigating organizational culture using quantitative methods.

Our approach to diagnosing and changing organizational culture offers six advantages:

- It is *practical:* It captures key dimensions of culture that have been found to make a difference in organizations' success.
- It is *timely:* The process of diagnosing and creating a strategy for change can be accomplished in a reasonable amount of time.
- It is *involving:* The steps in the process can include every member of the organization, but they especially involve all who have a responsibility to establish direction, reinforce values, and guide fundamental change.

- It is both *quantitative* and *qualitative*: The process relies on quantitative measurement of key cultural dimensions as well as qualitative methods including stories, incidents, and symbols that represent the unmeasurable ambience of the organization.

- It is *manageable*: The process of diagnosis and change can be undertaken and implemented by a team within the organization—usually the management team. Outside diagnosticians, culture experts, or change consultants are not required for successful implementation.

- It is *valid*: The framework on which the process is built not only makes sense to people as they consider their own organization but is also supported by an extensive empirical literature and underlying dimensions that have a verified scholarly foundation.

In other words, we do not claim that ours is the single best approach, but we do consider it a critically important strategy in an organization's repertoire for changing culture and improving performance.

Note

1. John Van Maanen of the Massachusetts Institute of Technology, one of the best researchers on organizational culture in the organizational sciences, aptly pointed out to us that "leaving readers with the suggestion that four and only four cultures represent the wonderful world of organizations is a mistake. One can almost hear our anthropological ancestors turning over in their graves." We want to communicate clearly that our theoretical model was developed in order to organize organizational culture types, but it does not pretend to be comprehensive of all cultural phenomena. Nor does it apply equally well to cultures at levels other than the organization level—for example, national cultures. The framework provides, instead, a way for or-

ganizations to discuss and interpret key elements of organizational culture that can foster change and improvement. A major problem in many organizations facing the need to change their cultures is that no language exists, no key elements or dimensions have been identified, and no common perspective is available to help the conversation even get started. Change doesn't occur because it is difficult to know what to talk about and what to focus on. In our experience, this framework provides an intuitively appealing and easily interpretable way to foster the process of culture change.

2

THE ORGANIZATIONAL CULTURE ASSESSMENT INSTRUMENT

In this chapter, we provide the Organizational Culture Assessment Instrument (OCAI), to be used to diagnose your organization's culture. The instrument is in the form of a questionnaire that requires individuals to respond to just six items. Longer versions of the OCAI containing more items have been developed (one is a twenty-four-item version), but the six items in this version have been found to be equally predictive of an organization's culture. Hence we prefer the more parsimonious version. Although there are a variety of ways to assess organizational culture (see Appendix A for a discussion), this instrument has been found to be both useful and accurate in diagnosing important aspects of an organization's underlying culture. It has been used in more than a thousand organizations that we know of, and it has been found to predict organizational performance. Its intent is to help identify the organization's current culture. That's step 1. The same instrument helps identify the culture that organization members think should be developed to match the future demands of the environment and the opportunities to be faced by the company. That's step 2.

We encourage you to take time now to answer the six questions for your own organization. Rate the organization in its current state, not as you'd like it to be. It will take about five minutes to complete the six questions. Use the "Now" column.

After you have completed the instrument, take another five minutes to complete the instrument a second time. This time, use the "Preferred" column. You should respond to the items as you would prefer your organization to be in five years. In other words, if your organization is to become even more excellent, if it is to achieve its highest aspirations, if it is to become an outstanding example of high performance, if it is to even outstrip the currently stated goals, if it is to be the benchmark for your industry, what should the culture be like?

We provide instructions for scoring the instrument and for creating an organizational culture profile for your company. In Chapter Five, we provide instructions for involving your entire organization in developing a more broad-based culture assessment as well as creating a strategy for cultural change.

Instructions for Diagnosing Organizational Culture

The purpose of the Organizational Culture Assessment Instrument is to assess six key dimensions of organizational culture. These dimensions are explained in some detail in Chapter Three. In completing the instrument, you will be providing a picture of the fundamental assumptions on which your organization operates and the values that characterize it. There are no right or wrong answers for these items, just as there is no right or wrong culture. Every organization will most likely be described by a different set of responses. Therefore, be as accurate as you can in responding to the items so that your resulting cultural diagnosis will be as precise as possible.

You are asked to rate your "organization" in the items. Of course, you may consider multiple organizations—your immediate team, your subunit, or the overall organization. To determine which is the best organization to rate, you will want to consider the organization that is managed by your boss, the strategic business unit to which you belong, or the organizational unit in which you are a member that has clearly identifiable boundaries. Because the instrument is most helpful for determining ways to change the culture, you'll want to *focus on the cultural unit that is the target for change*. For example, it may make little sense to try to describe the culture of the overall Ford Motor Company. It is simply too large and complex. The new product design unit is significantly different from a stamping plant or from the Customer Assistance Center. Therefore, as you answer the questions, keep in mind the organization that can be affected by your change strategy.

The OCAI consists of six items (see Figure 2.1). Each item has four alternatives. Divide 100 points among these four alternatives, depending on the extent to which each alternative is similar to your own organization. Give a higher number of points to the alternative that is most similar to your organization. For example, on item 1, if you think alternative A is very similar to your organization, alternatives B and C are somewhat similar, and alternative D is hardly similar at all, you might give 55 points to A, 20 points each to B and C, and 5 points to D. Just be sure that your total equals 100 for each item.

Note in Figure 2.1 that the left-hand response column for the instrument is labeled "Now." These responses mean that you are rating your organization as it is *currently*. Complete that rating first. When you have finished, think of your organization as you think it *should be in five years* in order to be spectacularly successful. Complete the instrument again, this time responding to the items as if your organization had achieved extraordinary success. Write these responses in the "Preferred" column. Your responses will thus produce two independent ratings of your organization's culture—one as it currently exists and one as you wish it to be in five years.

Scoring the OCAI

Scoring the OCAI is very easy. It requires simple arithmetic calculations. The first step is to add together all A responses in the "Now" column and divide by 6. That is, compute an average score for the A alternatives in the "Now" column. You may use the worksheet in Figure 2.2 if you'd like. Next, add together all B responses and divide by 6. Repeat this computation for the C and D alternatives.

Figure 2.1 The Organizational Culture Assessment
Instrument—Current Profile

1. Dominant Characteristics	Now	Preferred
A The organization is a very personal place. It is like an extended family. People seem to share a lot of themselves.		
B The organization is a very dynamic and entrepreneurial place. People are willing to stick their necks out and take risks.		
C The organization is very results-oriented. A major concern is with getting the job done. People are very competitive and achievement-oriented.		
D The organization is a very controlled and structured place. Formal procedures generally govern what people do.		
Total	100	100

2. Organizational Leadership	Now	Preferred
A The leadership in the organization is generally considered to exemplify mentoring, facilitating, or nurturing.		
B The leadership in the organization is generally considered to exemplify entrepreneurship, innovation, or risk taking.		
C The leadership in the organization is generally considered to exemplify a no-nonsense, aggressive, results-oriented focus.		
D The leadership in the organization is generally considered to exemplify coordinating, organizing, or smooth-running efficiency.		
Total	100	100

Figure 2.1 The Organizational Culture Assessment Instrument—Current Profile, Cont'd.

3. Management of Employees	Now	Preferred
A The management style in the organization is characterized by teamwork, consensus, and participation.		
B The management style in the organization is characterized by individual risk taking, innovation, freedom, and uniqueness.		
C The management style in the organization is characterized by hard-driving competitiveness, high demands, and achievement.		
D The management style in the organization is characterized by security of employment, conformity, predictability, and stability in relationships.		
Total	100	100

4. Organization Glue	Now	Preferred
A The glue that holds the organization together is loyalty and mutual trust. Commitment to this organization runs high.		
B The glue that holds the organization together is commitment to innovation and development. There is an emphasis on being on the cutting edge.		
C The glue that holds the organization together is the emphasis on achievement and goal accomplishment.		
D The glue that holds the organization together is formal rules and policies. Maintaining a smooth-running organization is important.		
Total	100	100

Figure 2.1 The Organizational Culture Assessment Instrument—Current Profile, Cont'd.

5. Strategic Emphases	Now	Preferred
A The organization emphasizes human development. High trust, openness, and participation persist.		
B The organization emphasizes acquiring new resources and creating new challenges. Trying new things and prospecting for opportunities are valued.		
C The organization emphasizes competitive actions and achievement. Hitting stretch targets and winning in the marketplace are dominant.		
D The organization emphasizes permanence and stability. Efficiency, control, and smooth operations are important.		
Total	100	100

6. Criteria of Success	Now	Preferred
A The organization defines success on the basis of the development of human resources, teamwork, employee commitment, and concern for people.		
B The organization defines success on the basis of having the most unique or newest products. It is a product leader and innovator.		
C The organization defines success on the basis of winning in the marketplace and outpacing the competition. Competitive market leadership is key.		
D The organization defines success on the basis of efficiency. Dependable delivery, smooth scheduling, and low-cost production are critical.		
Total	100	100

Figure 2.2 Worksheet for Scoring the OCAI

"Now" Scores

	1A
	2A
	3A
	4A
	5A
	6A
	Sum (total of A Responses)
	Average (sum divided by 6)

	1B
	2B
	3B
	4B
	5B
	6B
	Sum (total of B Responses)
	Average (sum divided by 6)

	1C
	2C
	3C
	4C
	5C
	6C
	Sum (total of C Responses)
	Average (sum divided by 6)

	1D
	2D
	3D
	4D
	5D
	6D
	Sum (total of D Responses)
	Average (sum divided by 6)

"Preferred" Scores

	1A
	2A
	3A
	4A
	5A
	6A
	Sum (total of A Responses)
	Average (sum divided by 6)

	1B
	2B
	3B
	4B
	5B
	6B
	Sum (total of B Responses)
	Average (sum divided by 6)

	1C
	2C
	3C
	4C
	5C
	6C
	Sum (total of C Responses)
	Average (sum divided by 6)

	1D
	2D
	3D
	4D
	5D
	6D
	Sum (total of D Responses)
	Average (sum divided by 6)

The second step is to add all A responses in the "Preferred" column and divide by 6. In other words, compute an average score for the A alternatives in the "Preferred" column. Again, use the worksheet in Figure 2.2 if you'd like. Next, add together all B responses and divide by 6. Repeat this computation for the C and D alternatives.

Following an explanation in Chapter Three of the framework on which the OCAI is based, we explain in Chapter Four the meaning of your average A, B, C, and D scores. Each of these scores relates to a type of organizational culture. In Chapter Four, we also provide a worksheet for you to plot these scores or to draw a picture of your organization's culture. This plot serves as an organizational culture profile and is an important step in initiating a culture change strategy.

3

THE COMPETING
VALUES FRAMEWORK

The OCAI is based on a theoretical model known as the *Competing Values Framework*. This framework is extremely useful in organizing and interpreting a wide variety of organizational phenomena. In this chapter, we explain why having a framework is so important and how this framework was initially developed through research on organizational effectiveness. We also explain the four dominant culture types that emerge from the framework. These four culture types serve as the foundation for the OCAI. In addition, because culture defines the core values, assumptions, interpretations, and approaches that characterize an organization, we might expect that other characteristics of organizations would also reflect the four culture types. We point out examples of how this is the case. In particular, we show how the Competing Values Framework is useful for identifying the major approaches to organizational design, stages of life cycle development, organizational quality, theories of effectiveness, leadership roles and roles of human resource managers, and management skills.

The Value of Frameworks

In the last couple of decades, writers have proposed a variety of dimensions and attributes of organizational culture. Detailed reviews of much of that literature can be found in Cameron and Ettington (1988), Martin (1992), Trice and Beyer (1993), and Beyer and Cameron (1997). To illustrate the variety of dimensions represented, a few are mentioned here. For example, Sathe (1983), Schein

(1984), and Kotter and Heskett (1992) are among those who argued for cultural strength and congruence as the main cultural dimensions of interest. Alpert and Whetten (1985) identified a holographic versus idiographic dimension as critical when analyzing culture. Arnold and Capella (1985) proposed a strong-weak dimension and an internal-external focus dimension. Deal and Kennedy (1983) proposed a dimension based on speed of feedback (high speed to low speed) and a degree-of-risk dimension (high risk to low risk). Ernst (1985) argued for people orientation (participative versus nonparticipative) and response to the environment (reactive versus proactive) as the key culture dimensions. Gordon (1985) identified eleven dimensions of culture: clarity and direction, organizational reach, integration, top management contact, encouragement of individual initiative, conflict resolution, performance clarity, performance emphasis, action orientation, compensation, and human resource development. Hofstede (1980) focused on power distance, uncertainty avoidance, individualism, and masculinity, and Kets de Vries and Miller (1986) focused on dysfunctional dimensions of culture, including paranoid, avoidant, charismatic, bureaucratic, and politicized dimensions. Martin (1992) proposed cultural integration and consensus, differentiation and conflict, and fragmentation and ambiguity.[1]

One reason so many dimensions have been proposed is that organizational culture is extremely broad and inclusive in scope. It comprises a complex, interrelated, comprehensive, and ambiguous set of factors. Consequently, it is impossible to ever include every relevant factor in diagnosing and assessing organizational culture. One more element can always be argued to be relevant. To determine the most important dimensions on which to focus, therefore, it is important to use an underlying framework, a theoretical foundation that can narrow and focus the search for key cultural dimensions. No one framework is comprehensive, of course, nor can one particular framework be argued to be right while others are wrong. Rather, the most appropriate frameworks should be based on empirical evidence, should capture accurately the reality being described (in other words, they should be valid), and should be able to integrate and organize most of the dimensions being proposed. That is the purpose of using the Competing Values Framework to diagnose and facilitate change in organizational culture. It is a framework that was empirically derived, has been found to have both face and empirical validity, and helps integrate many of the dimensions proposed by various authors. A more detailed discussion of why this is so is found in Cameron and Ettington (1988, pp. 369–373) and Quinn (1988, pp. 34–38 and 46–50).

In brief, the Competing Values Framework has been found to have a high degree of congruence with well-known and well-accepted categorical schemes that organize the way people think, their values and assumptions, and the ways they process information. That is, similar categorical schemes have been proposed independently by a variety of psychologists, among them Jung (1923), Myers and Briggs (1962), McKenney and Keen (1974), Mason and Mitroff (1973), and Mitroff and Kilmann (1978). This congruence of frameworks occurs because of an underlying similarity in people at the deep psychological level of their cognitive processes. Mitroff (1983, p. 5) put it this way:

> The more that one examines the great diversity of world cultures, the more one finds that at the symbolic level there is an astounding amount of agreement between various archetypal images. People may disagree and fight one another by day but at night they show the most profound similarity in their dreams and myths. The agreement is too profound to be produced by chance alone. It is therefore attributed to a similarity of the psyche at the deepest layers of the unconscious. These similar-appearing symbolic images are termed archetypes.

Development of the Competing Values Framework

The Competing Values Framework was developed initially from research conducted on the major indicators of effective organizations. The key questions asked in the investigation were these: What are the main criteria for determining if an organization is effective or not? What key factors define organizational effectiveness? When people judge an organization to be effective, what indicators do they have in mind? John Campbell and his colleagues (1974) created a list of thirty-nine indicators that they claimed represented a comprehensive set of all possible measures for organizational effectiveness. That list of indicators was analyzed by Quinn and Rohrbaugh (1983) to determine if patterns or clusters could be identified. Since thirty-nine indicators are too many to comprehend or to be useful in organizations, they sought a more parsimonious way to identify the key factors of effectiveness.

Those thirty-nine indicators of effectiveness were submitted to a statistical analysis, and two major dimensions emerged that organized the indicators into four main clusters. (See Appendix A for a more detailed explanation of the statistical analyses in this and other studies of this framework.) One dimension differentiates effectiveness criteria that emphasize flexibility, discretion, and dynamism from criteria that emphasize stability, order, and control. That is, some organizations are viewed as effective if they are changing, adaptable, and organic—for example, neither the product mix nor the organizational form stays in place very long at firms such as Microsoft or Nike. Other organizations are viewed as effective if they are stable, predictable, and mechanistic—for example, most universities, government agencies, and conglomerates such as Boeing are characterized by longevity and staying power in both design and outputs. The continuum ranges from organizational versatility and pliability on one end to organizational steadiness and durability on the other end.

The second dimension differentiates effectiveness criteria that emphasize an internal orientation, integration, and unity from criteria that emphasize an external orientation, differentiation, and rivalry. That is, some organizations are viewed as effective if they have harmonious internal characteristics—for example, IBM and Hewlett-Packard have traditionally been recognized for a consistent "IBM way" or the "H-P way." Others are judged to be effective if they are focused on interacting or competing with others outside their boundaries—for example, Toyota and Honda are known for "thinking globally but acting locally," that is, for having units adopt the attributes of the local environment more than a centrally prescribed approach. The continuum ranges from organizational cohesion and consonance on the one end to organizational separation and independence on the other.

Together these two dimensions form four quadrants, each representing a distinct set of organizational effectiveness indicators. Figure 3.1 illustrates the relationships of these two dimensions to one another. These indicators of effectiveness represent what people value about an organization's performance. They define what is seen as good and right and appropriate. The four clusters of criteria, in other words, define the core values on which judgments about organizations are made.

What is notable about these four core values is that they represent opposite or competing assumptions. Each continuum highlights a core value that is opposite from the value on the other end

Figure 3.1 The Competing Values Framework

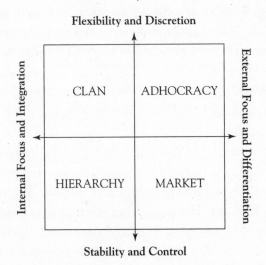

of the continuum—flexibility versus stability, internal versus external. The dimensions therefore produce quadrants that are also contradictory or competing on the diagonal. The upper left quadrant, for example, identifies values that emphasize an internal, organic focus, whereas the lower right quadrant identifies values that emphasize an external, control focus. Similarly, the upper right quadrant identifies values that emphasize an external, organic focus, whereas the lower left quadrant emphasizes internal, control values. The competing or opposite values in each quadrant give rise to the name for the model, the Competing Values Framework.

Each quadrant in Figure 3.1 has been given a label to distinguish its most notable characteristics—*clan, adhocracy, market,* and *hierarchy.* The clan quadrant is in the upper left, the adhocracy quadrant is in the upper right, the hierarchy quadrant is in the lower left, and the market quadrant is in the lower right. It is important to note that these quadrant names were not randomly selected. Rather, they were derived from the scholarly literature that explains how, over time, different organizational values have become associated with different forms of organizations. We discovered that the four quadrants that emerged from these analyses match precisely the main organizational forms that have developed in organizational science. They also match key management theories about organizational success, approaches to organizational quality, leadership roles, and management skills. Moreover, in past research on child development (such as that of Piaget, 1932), cognitive maps (Hampton-Turner, 1981), and information processing (Mitroff, 1983), similar dimensions have emerged that help organize the way in which the brain and body work as well as the way behavior is organized.

The dimensions and quadrants in Figure 3.1 appear to be very robust in explaining the different orientations, as well as the competing values, that characterize human behavior. The robustness of these dimensions and the richness of the resulting quadrants led us to identify each quadrant as a cultural type. That is, each quadrant represents basic assumptions, orientations, and values—the same elements that comprise an organizational culture. The OCAI, therefore, is an instrument that allows you to diagnose the dominant orientation of your own organization based on these core culture types. It also assists you in diagnosing your organization's cultural strength, cultural type, and cultural congruence.

The Four Major Culture Types

We shall now explain and illustrate each of the four culture types.

The Hierarchy Culture

The earliest approach to organizing in the modern era was based on the work of a German sociologist, Max Weber, who studied government organizations in Europe during the early 1900s The major challenge faced by organizations at the turn of the twentieth century was to efficiently produce goods and services for an increasingly complex society. To accomplish this, Weber (1947) proposed seven characteristics that have become known as the classical attributes of bureaucracy: rules, specialization, meritocracy, hierarchy, separate ownership, impersonality, accountability. These characteristics were highly effective in accomplishing their purpose. They were adopted widely in organizations whose major challenge was to generate efficient, reliable, smooth-flowing, predictable output. In fact, until the 1960s, almost every book on management and organizational studies made the assumption that Weber's hierarchy or bureaucracy was the ideal form of organization because it led to stable, efficient, highly consistent products and services. Because the environment was relatively stable, tasks and functions could be integrated and coordinated, uniformity in products and services was maintained, and workers and jobs were under control. Clear lines of decision-making authority, standardized rules and procedures, and control and accountability mechanisms were valued as the keys to success.

The organizational culture compatible with this form (and as assessed in the OCAI) is characterized by a formalized and structured place to work. Procedures govern what people do. Effective leaders are good coordinators and organizers. Maintaining a smooth-running organization is important. The long-term concerns of the organization are stability, predictability, and efficiency. Formal rules and policies hold the organization together.

Organizations ranging from a typical U.S. fast-food restaurant (such as McDonald's) to major conglomerates (like Ford Motor Company) and government agencies (such as the Justice Department) provide prototypical examples of a hierarchy culture. Large organizations and government agencies are generally dominated by a hierarchy culture, as evidenced by large numbers of standardized procedures, multiple hierarchical levels (Ford has seventeen levels of management), and an emphasis on rule reinforcement. Even in small organizations such as a McDonald's restaurant, however, a hierarchy culture can dominate. For example, many of the employees in the typical McDonald's restaurant are young people who have no previous training or work experience, and a hallmark of the business is the uniformity of products in all outlets. Key values center on maintaining efficient, reliable, fast, smooth-flowing production. New employees begin by doing only one specific job (such as cooking french fries). Almost no discretion is provided by the job, since uncooked fries are shipped from a central supplier in standardized packages, the temperature of the oil is predetermined, and a buzzer tells employees when to take the fries out. The rules specify that only a certain number of seconds can elapse from when the buzzer goes off to when the fries must be removed from the oil. And they may sit under the heat lamp for only a certain time as well. The rules manual, which every employee studies and is tested on, is over 350 pages long and covers most aspects of employee dress and on-the-job behavior. One requirement for promotion is knowledge of these rules and policies. Promotion within the restaurant follows a specific series of steps, and it is possible for an employee to be promoted several times within a restaurant before reaching a managerial level (for example, from fry cook to hamburger cook to counter person to crew chief to assistant manager).

The Market Culture

Another form of organizing became popular during the late 1960s as organizations faced new competitive challenges. This form relied on a fundamentally different set of assumptions than the hierarchy and was based largely on the work of Oliver Williamson (1975), Bill Ouchi (1981), and their colleagues. These organizational scholars identified an alternative set of activities that they argued served as the foundation of organizational effectiveness. The most important of these was transaction costs.

The new design was referred to as a *market* form of organization. The term *market* is not synonymous with the marketing function or with consumers in the marketplace. Rather, it refers to a type of organization that functions as a market itself. It is oriented toward the external environment instead of internal affairs. It is focused on transactions with (mainly) external constituencies such as suppliers, customers, contractors, licensees, unions, and regulators. And unlike a hierarchy, where internal control is maintained by rules, specialized jobs, and centralized decisions, the market operates primarily through economic market mechanisms, mainly monetary exchange. That is, the major focus of markets is to conduct transactions (exchanges, sales, contracts) with other constituencies to create competitive advantage. Profitability, bottom-line results, strength in market niches, stretch targets, and secure customer bases are primary objectives of the organization. Not surprisingly, the core values that dominate market-type organizations are competitiveness and productivity.

Competitiveness and productivity in market organizations are achieved through a strong emphasis on external positioning and control (the lower right quadrant of Figure 3.1). At Philips Electronics, for example, the loss of market share in Europe and a first-ever year of red ink in 1991 led to a corporationwide initiative to improve the competitive position of the firm. Under the leadership of a new CEO, the worldwide organization instituted a process called Centurion in which a concerted effort was made to shift the company's culture from a relatively complacent, arrogant, hierarchy culture to a culture driven by customer focus, premium returns on assets, and improved corporate competitiveness—a market culture. Three yearly meetings were held to assess performance and to establish new stretch targets. Assessments using the OCAI showed a substantial shift toward a market-driven culture from the early 1990s to the mid-1990s.

A similar example of a market culture is a Philips competitor, General Electric. General Electric's former CEO, Jack Welch, made it clear in the late 1980s that if GE businesses were not number one or number two in their markets, they would be sold. Welch bought and sold over three hundred businesses during his twenty-one year tenure as CEO. The GE culture under Welch was known as a highly competitive, results-or-else, take-no-prisoners type of culture. It reflected a stereotypical market culture.

The basic assumptions in a market culture are that the external environment is not benign but hostile, consumers are choosy and interested in value, the organization is in the business of increasing its competitive position, and the major task of management is to drive the organization toward productivity, results, and profits. It is assumed that a clear purpose and an aggressive strategy lead to productivity and profitability. In the words of General George Patton (1944), market organizations "are not interested in holding on to [their] positions. Let the [enemy] do that. [They] are advancing all the time, defeating the opposition, marching constantly toward the goal."

A market culture, as assessed in the OCAI, is a results-oriented workplace. Leaders are hard-driving producers and competitors. They are tough and demanding. The glue that holds the organization together is an emphasis on winning. The long-term concern is on competitive actions and achieving stretch goals and targets. Success is defined in terms of market share and penetration. Outpacing the competition and market leadership are important.

The Clan Culture

A third ideal form of organization is represented by the upper left quadrant in Figure 3.1. It is called a *clan* because of its similarity to a family-type organization. After studying Japanese firms in the late 1960s and early 1970s, a number of researchers observed fundamental differences between the market and hierarchy forms of design in America and clan forms of design in Japan (Ouchi, 1981; Pascale and Athos, 1981; Lincoln, 2003). Shared values and goals, cohesion, participativeness, individuality, and a sense of "we-ness" permeated clan-type firms. They seemed more like extended families than economic entities. Instead of the rules and procedures of hierarchies or the competitive profit centers of markets, typical characteristics of clan-type firms were teamwork, employee involvement programs, and corporate commitment to employees. These characteristics were evidenced by semiautonomous work teams that received rewards on the basis of team (not individual) accomplishment and that hired and fired their own members, quality circles that encouraged workers to voice suggestions regarding how to improve their own work and the performance of the company, and an empowering environment for employees.

Some basic assumptions in a clan culture are that the environment can best be managed through teamwork and employee development, customers are best thought of as partners, the organization is in the business of developing a humane work environment, and the major task of management is to empower employees and facilitate their participation, commitment, and loyalty.

These characteristics are not new to American organizations, of course. They have been advocated for decades by many writers associated with the human relations movement (McGregor, 1960; Likert, 1970; Argyris, 1964). However, it took the highly visible success of Japanese firms, which had adopted these principles and applied them successfully after World War II, to help U.S. and Western European organizations catch the message in the late 1970s and 1980s that clan cultures can make good business sense. For example, when rapidly changing, turbulent environments make it difficult for managers to plan far in advance and when decision making is uncertain, it was found that an effective way to coordinate organizational activity is to make certain that all employees share the same values, beliefs, and goals. In the post–World War II environment, Japanese organizations caught the message long before Western organizations did.

An example of a clan-type organization in the United States was PeopleExpress Airlines in its first five years of operation—until its founder, Don Burr, encountered financial difficulties that led him to sell the company to avoid bankruptcy. After leaving Texas Air in 1980, Burr dreamed of creating not just a profitable airline but a model of how ideal organizations ought to function. Burr brought with him several other officials from Texas Air and within two years had defied all experts' predictions by turning a profit—the most dramatic success story in the history of the airline industry.

The hallmark characteristics of PeopleExpress were (1) minimal management levels—only three levels of management existed between Burr and flight deck personnel; (2) informality and self-management—Burr's office doubled as the conference room, and when it was being used, he went someplace else; (3) employee ownership—all employees owned company stock and had lifetime job security; (4) work teams—the entire workforce was organized into teams of three or four people, mostly self-selected; (5) participation— at least four separate management councils helped make company decisions; and (6) job rotation—employees regularly switched jobs so that pilots were, for example, also baggage handlers and reservations hosts. Fierce loyalty to Burr and to the concept of PeopleExpress kept employees' salaries far below rival airlines while morale initially remained high. As indicated by these characteristics, PeopleExpress was clearly organized on the basis of the clan model. The incompatibility of this clan culture with the kind of company that was created when the highly unionized and adversarial Frontier Airlines was merged with PeopleExpress led to the airline's downfall.

The clan culture, as assessed in the OCAI, is typified by a friendly place to work where people share a lot of themselves. It is like an extended family. Leaders are thought of as mentors and perhaps even as parent figures. The organization is held together by loyalty and tradition. Commitment is high. The organization emphasizes the long-term benefit of individual development, with high cohesion and morale being important. Success is defined in terms of internal climate and concern for people. The organization places a premium on teamwork, participation, and consensus.

The Adhocracy Culture

As the developed world shifted from the industrial age to the information age, a fourth ideal type of organizing emerged. It is an organizational form that is most responsive to the hyperturbulent, ever-accelerating conditions that increasingly typify the organizational world of the twenty-first century. With rapidly decreasing half-life of product and service advantages, a set of assumptions were developed that differed from those of the other three forms of organization. These assumptions were that innovative and pioneering initiatives are what leads to success, that organizations are mainly in the business of developing new products and services and preparing for the future, and that the major task of management is to foster entrepreneurship, creativity, and activity "on the cutting edge." It was assumed that adaptation and innovativeness lead to new resources and profitability, so emphasis was placed on creating a vision of the future, organized anarchy, and disciplined imagination.

The root of the word *adhocracy* is *ad hoc*—implying something temporary, specialized, and dynamic. Most people have served on an ad hoc task force or committee, which disbands as soon as its task is completed. Adhocracies are similarly temporary. They have been characterized as "tents rather than palaces" in that they can reconfigure themselves rapidly when new circumstances arise. A major goal of an adhocracy is to foster adaptability, flexibility, and creativity where uncertainty, ambiguity, and information overload are typical.

The adhocracy organization may frequently be found in industries such as aerospace, software development, think-tank consulting, and filmmaking. An important challenge for these organizations is to produce innovative products and services and to adapt quickly to new opportunities. Unlike markets or hierarchies, adhocracies do not have centralized power or authority relationships. Instead, power flows from individual to individual or from task team to task team, depending on what problem is being addressed at the time. Emphasis on individuality, risk taking, and anticipating the future is high as almost everyone in an adhocracy becomes involved with production, clients, research and development, and other matters. For example, each different client demand in a consulting firm is treated as an independent project, and a temporary organizational design is set up to accomplish the task. When the project ends, the structure disintegrates.

Similarly, the story of the successful failure of the Apollo 13 space mission illustrates clearly how leadership changes regularly and often unpredictably, team membership is temporary, and no clear map can be drawn to identify the communication or control system. During the flight, astronauts in the space capsule as well as support personnel on the ground were not organized in a stable way for very long. Different problems demanded different types of task teams to address them, leadership shifted often, and even the piloting of the spacecraft switched from one astronaut to another. This was typical of the entire Manned Space Flight Center at NASA. Its formal structure changed seventeen times in the first eight years of its existence. No organizational chart was ever drawn because it would have been outdated before it could be printed. Jurisdictional lines, precedents, and policies were treated as temporary. Titles, job responsibilities, and even departmental alignments changed, sometimes weekly. The organization operated with an adhocratic design and reflected values typical of an adhocracy culture.

Sometimes adhocratic subunits exist in larger organizations that have a dominant culture of a different type. For example, an adhocracy subunit culture existing within a hierarchy was described in a study we conducted of the evolutionary changes that occurred in the Department of Mental Hygiene in the state government of New York (Quinn and Cameron, 1983). In its first five years of existence, the department was organized as an adhocracy. Among the characteristics we found in our analysis were the following: (1) no organizational chart—it was impossible to draw an organizational chart because it changed frequently and rapidly; (2) temporary physical space—the director did not have an office and set up temporary bases of operations wherever he thought he was needed; (3) temporary roles—staff members were assigned and reassigned different responsibilities, depending on changing client problems; and (4) creativity and innovation—employees were encouraged to formulate innovative solutions to problems and to generate new ways of providing services to clients. Because this adhocracy was so inconsistent with the larger state government design (a hierarchy) and with an environment that demanded efficiency and accountability, it was forced to shift to another type of culture. Similar shifts are typical in many organizations, and we discuss them in the next section.

In sum, the adhocracy culture, as assessed in the OCAI, is characterized by a dynamic, entrepreneurial, and creative workplace. People stick their necks out and take risks. Effective leadership is visionary, innovative, and risk-oriented. The glue that holds the organization together is commitment to experimentation and innovation. The emphasis is on being at the leading edge of new knowledge, products, and services. Readiness for change and meeting new challenges are important. The organization's long-term emphasis is on rapid growth and acquiring new resources. Success means producing unique and original products and services.

Applicability of the Competing Values Model

As we have studied various aspects of organizations and worked with organizations in the process of change, we have discovered that the Competing Values Framework also orders attributes of organizations in addition to cultural values and forms of organizing. Because the framework was formulated on the basis of very fundamental assumptions about how organizations work and how they are managed, it is not surprising that such a robust framework would accurately describe other aspects of organizations as well. Figure 3.2 lists the leadership roles, the effectiveness criteria, and the core management theories most closely associated with each of the four quadrants.

Organizational Leadership

Our own research has discovered that most organizations develop a dominant cultural style. More than 80 percent of the several thousand organizations we have studied have been characterized by one

Figure 3.2   The Competing Values of Leadership, Effectiveness, and Organizational Theory

Flexibility and Discretion

Culture Type: CLAN	**Culture Type: ADHOCRACY**
Orientation: COLLABORATIVE	**Orientation:** CREATIVE
Leader Type: Facilitator	**Leader Type:** Innovator
Mentor	Entrepreneur
Team builder	Visionary
Value Drivers: Commitment	**Value Drivers:** Innovative outputs
Communication	Transformation
Development	Agility
Theory of Human development	**Theory of** Innovativeness, vision,
Effectiveness: and participation produce effectiveness.	**Effectiveness:** and new resources produce effectiveness.
Culture Type: HIERARCHY	**Culture Type: MARKET**
Orientation: CONTROLLING	**Orientation:** COMPETING
Leader Type: Coordinator	**Leader Type:** Hard driver
Monitor	Competitor
Organizer	Producer
Value Drivers: Efficiency	**Value Drivers:** Market share
Timeliness	Goal achievement
Consistency and uniformity	Profitability
Theory of Control and efficiency	**Theory of** Aggressively competing
Effectiveness: with capable processes produce effectiveness.	**Effectiveness:** and customer focus produce effectiveness.

Internal Focus and Integration

External Focus and Differentiation

Stability and Control

or more of the culture types identified by the framework. Those that do not have a dominant culture type either tend to be unclear about their culture or emphasize the four different cultural types nearly equally. When an organization is dominated by the hierarchy culture, for example, we have found that the most effective managers—those rated as most successful by their subordinates, peers, and superiors and those who tend to move up quickly in the organization—demonstrate a matching leadership style. That is, they are good at organizing, controlling, monitoring, administering, coordinating, and maintaining efficiency. When an organization is dominated by the market culture, the managers rated as most effective tend to be hard-driving, whip-cracking, backside-kicking competitors. They are good at directing, producing results, negotiating, and motivating others. When the organization is dominated by the clan culture, the most effective leaders are parent figures, team builders, facilitators, nurturers, mentors, and supporters. Effective leaders in organizations dominated by the adhocracy culture tend to be entrepreneurial, visionary, innovative, creative, risk-oriented, and focused on the future. It is easy to see, of course, that the most effective leadership styles tend to match the organization's culture. Moreover, the dominant styles in the diagonal quadrants are opposite from one another. Adhocracy leaders are rule breakers, for example, whereas hierarchy leaders are rule reinforcers. Clan leaders are warm and supportive, whereas market leaders are tough and demanding.

Parenthetically, we have also discovered that the highest-performing leaders, those rated by their peers, superiors, and subordinates as the most highly effective, have developed capabilities and skills that allow them to succeed in each of the four quadrants (Denison, Hooijberg, & Quinn, 1995). That is, they are self-contradictory leaders in the sense that they can be simultaneously hard and soft, entrepreneurial and controlled. Managerial effectiveness, as well as organizational effectiveness, is inherently tied to paradoxical attributes (Cameron, 1984, 1986; Quinn & Cameron, 1988).

In addition to the roles of leaders, the managerial leadership skills possessed by those involved in the culture change process also have an important relationship to personal and organizational effectiveness. Chapter Six is devoted to an explanation of the key skills managers must demonstrate and improve to be personally effective and, more important, to facilitate organizational culture change. A diagnostic instrument is provided to help managers determine their own managerial strengths and weaknesses and develop a personal improvement agenda.

Organizational Effectiveness

The criteria of effectiveness most highly valued in a hierarchy culture are efficiency, timeliness, smooth functioning, and predictability. The dominant operational theory that drives organizational success is that control fosters efficiency (elimination of waste and redundancy) and therefore effectiveness. Hierarchy organizations, like the Internal Revenue Service, for example, are judged to be effective only if they achieve these dominant characteristics. We don't want flexibility in the IRS; we want error-free efficiency.

The criteria of effectiveness most highly valued in a market culture are achieving goals, outpacing the competition, increasing market share, and acquiring premium levels of financial return. The dominant operational theory that drives organizational success is that competition creates an impetus for higher levels of productivity and therefore higher levels of effectiveness. The all-out assault of the Big Three automobile companies in North America—General Motors, Ford, and DaimlerChrysler—on foreign competitors—especially Toyota, Nissan, and Honda—during the 1990s is an illustration. Anything short of recapturing market share, enhancing revenues, and increasing productivity was seen as failure.

In a clan culture, the criteria of effectiveness most highly valued include cohesion, high levels of employee morale and satisfaction, human resource development, and teamwork. The operational theory that dominates this culture type is that involvement and participation of employees foster empowerment and commitment. Committed, satisfied employees produce effectiveness. The care taken by the Disney corporation, for example, to integrate each employee into the "cast"—even requiring that they know the traditions of the family so well that they can name the seven dwarfs in the Snow White story—illustrates the basic theory that committed employees produce world-class results.

Finally, the adhocracy culture most highly values new products, creative solutions to problems, cutting-edge ideas, and growth in new markets as the dominant effectiveness criteria. The underlying operational theory is that innovation and new ideas create new markets, new customers, and new opportunities. These outcomes comprise the basic indicators of effective performance. When IBM was challenged by a more innovative and agile Apple Computer Company in the 1980s, IBM was stereotyped as sluggish, cumbersome, and elitist. Apple's success, as a result of innovative hardware and software, was dramatic. In the 1990s, however, Apple lost its competitive edge—producing few new products, having slower time to market, being less innovative—whereas IBM recaptured some of its lost luster and nearly drove Apple out of business by committing significant resources to innovative products and new technologies (such as networking on the Internet). The IBM-Apple war, trumpeted on the cover of *Fortune* in the late 1980s, has been won by the more innovative competitor.

Total Quality Management

The Competing Values Framework is also helpful in organizing the various aspects of total quality management (TQM) and highlighting its comprehensive nature. An extensive literature exists on the topic of TQM. It ranges from descriptions of quality tools and techniques (statistical process control, quality function deployment, Pareto charting) to philosophical discussions of the nature of management (Deming's fourteen points). One review of the TQM literature pointed out that a large percentage of total quality initiatives fail (Cameron, 1997). Either quality does not improve, or the initiatives are abandoned after a short time. Two of the major reasons for this failure are partial deployment and failure to integrate TQM and culture change. Partial deployment means that only a limited number of aspects of TQM are implemented. For example, many organizations create teams or gather customer satisfaction data but not much else. Or some organizations implement new statistical controls or redesign processes to prevent defects, but little else changes. Figure 3.3 uses the Competing Values Framework to highlight a more comprehensive set of TQM factors. When all of these are integrated in a TQM project, the success rate increases significantly.

Figure 3.3 The Competing Values of Total Quality Management

Flexibility and Discretion

Internal Focus and Integration

External Focus and Differentiation

CLAN

QUALITY STRATEGIES
Empowerment
Team building
Employee involvement
Human resource development
Open communication

ADHOCRACY

QUALITY STRATEGIES
Surprise and delight
Creating new standards
Anticipating needs
Continuous improvement
Finding creative solutions

HIERARCHY

QUALITY STRATEGIES
Error detection
Measurement
Process control
Systematic problem solving
Quality tools (fishbone diagrams,
Pareto charting, affinity
graphing, variance plotting)

MARKET

QUALITY STRATEGIES
Measuring customer preferences
Improving productivity
Creating external partnerships
Enhancing competitiveness
Involving customers and suppliers

Stability and Control

For example, to foster the highest levels of quality in organizations requires the application of a variety of hierarchy culture activities such as improving measurement, process control, and systematic problem solving. It involves tools such as Pareto charting, fishbone diagramming, affinity charts, and variance plots. These are commonly known and applied quality tools. However, world-class quality also requires the application of market culture activities such as measuring customer preferences before and after product and service delivery, improving productivity, creating partnerships with suppliers and customers, and enhancing competitiveness by involving customers in planning and design. It must include clan culture activities such as empowerment, team building, employee involvement, human resource development, and open communication. A common adage is that firms cannot treat customers any better than they treat their employees. TQM must also include adhocracy activities such as surprising and delighting customers, creating new standards of performance, anticipating customer needs, engaging in continuous improvement, and implementing creative solutions to problems that produce new customer preferences. In most failed TQM attempts (which constitute a majority), the elements of each of the four quadrants are not implemented; only a partial approach is tried. In other words, the Competing Values Framework helps us identify a more comprehensive approach to quality because it highlights the key elements of the four main cultures that underlie organizational performance.

Human Resource Management Roles

Our colleague David Ulrich has conducted comprehensive studies of human resource (HR) management. In summarizing some of those findings, the Competing Values Framework was used to identify the changing roles of the human resource manager. Figure 3.4 summarizes his conclusions (see Ulrich and Brockbank, 2005).

Figure 3.4 The Competing Values of Human Resource Management

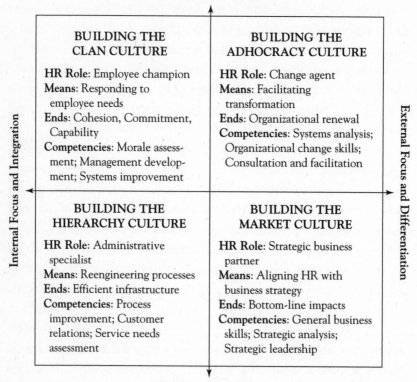

Flexibility and Discretion

Internal Focus and Integration

External Focus and Differentiation

BUILDING THE CLAN CULTURE

HR Role: Employee champion
Means: Responding to employee needs
Ends: Cohesion, Commitment, Capability
Competencies: Morale assessment; Management development; Systems improvement

BUILDING THE ADHOCRACY CULTURE

HR Role: Change agent
Means: Facilitating transformation
Ends: Organizational renewal
Competencies: Systems analysis; Organizational change skills; Consultation and facilitation

BUILDING THE HIERARCHY CULTURE

HR Role: Administrative specialist
Means: Reengineering processes
Ends: Efficient infrastructure
Competencies: Process improvement; Customer relations; Service needs assessment

BUILDING THE MARKET CULTURE

HR Role: Strategic business partner
Means: Aligning HR with business strategy
Ends: Bottom-line impacts
Competencies: General business skills; Strategic analysis; Strategic leadership

Stability and Control

In brief, Figure 3.4 points out the different roles, skills, and activities required to adequately manage the human resource function in a large organization. The effective HR manager must ensure, according to Ulrich's research, that some elements of each of the four cultures is represented in the organization. More important, the roles, means, ends, and competencies emphasized by the HR manager must reinforce the dominant or desired culture of the firm. Displaying different HR roles can help build or strengthen a different kind of organizational culture. For example, building or strengthening a hierarchy culture requires an administrative specialist who focuses on reengineering processes and creating an efficient infrastructure. Building or strengthening a market culture requires the human resource manager to be a strategic business partner in the organization, aligning HR with business strategy and facilitating bottom-line (financial) impacts of all HR activities. Building or strengthening a clan culture requires an employee champion who responds to employee needs and fosters commitment and human capability in the workforce. Building or strengthening an adhocracy culture requires a change agent who facilitates transformational change and organizational renewal.

The point is that this framework highlights a rather comprehensive view of human resource management—more comprehensive than appears in much of the HR literature—and shows how organizational change and improvement can be fostered by the human resource manager. It provides a way to make the HR function more strategic, more inclusive, and more rational.

Culture Change over Time

Another discovery emerging from our research on this framework is that new or small organizations tend to progress through a predictable pattern of organization culture changes (see, for example, Quinn and Cameron, 1983). Think of almost any new organization you know that began small and grew larger over time. See if the following description and illustrations don't match your own experience.

In the earliest stages of the organizational life cycle, organizations tend to be dominated by the adhocracy quadrant—without formal structure and characterized by entrepreneurship. They are largely devoid of formal policies and structures, and they are often led by a single, powerful, visionary leader. As they develop over time, they supplement that orientation with a clan culture—a family feeling, a strong sense of belonging, and personal identification with the organization. Organization members get many of their social and emotional needs fulfilled in the organization, and a sense of community and personal friendship exists. A potential crisis frequently arises, however, as the organization grows. It eventually finds itself faced with the need to emphasize structure and standard procedures in order to control the expanding responsibilities. Order and predictability are needed, so a shift to a hierarchy culture occurs. That reorientation frequently makes organization members feel that the organization has lost the friendly, personal feeling that once characterized the workplace, and personal satisfaction decreases. The hierarchy orientation is eventually supplemented by a focus on the market culture—competitiveness, achieving results, and an emphasis on external relationships. The focus shifts from impersonality and formal control inside the organization to a customer orientation and competition outside the organization. It is the case, of course, that mature and highly effective organizations tend to develop subunits or segments that represent each of these four culture types. R&D may be adhocratic, for example, whereas accounting may be hierarchical in culture emphasis. Almost always, however, one or more of the culture types dominate an organization.

An example of this life cycle shift in culture can be illustrated by describing briefly the development of Apple Computer Company. Steven Jobs and Steven Wozniak invented the first personal computer in the garage of Jobs's parents' home. Apple Computer Company was subsequently formed to produce personal computers with young, dynamic, unconstrained California folks who prided themselves on being free of policy manuals and rule books. The culture was characterized by Profile 1 in Figure 3.5. As is typical of most adhocracies, a single entrepreneurial, charismatic leader was setting direction, and the company was flexible and freewheeling. The press described the group as "renegades and crazies."

This cultural profile was produced from the Organizational Culture Assessment Instrument described in Chapter Two. The high degree of emphasis in the Adhocracy quadrant, moderate scores in the Clan quadrant, and low scores in the Hierarchy and Market quadrants produce the profile illustrated in Profile 1. Apple's culture was dominated by an entrepreneurial, innovative, adhocractic culture.

Figure 3.5 The Life Cycle of Apple Computer Company

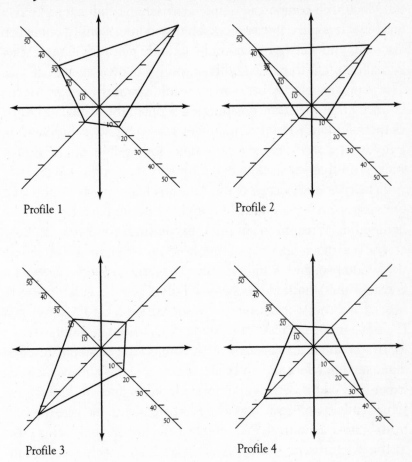

Profile 1

Profile 2

Profile 3

Profile 4

Within a few of years of incorporation, Apple established one of the most successful ventures ever experienced in the industry—the formation of a group of "pirates," dubbed the Macintosh Team. This team of selected employees was charged with developing a computer that people would want to purchase for use in their homes. Until then, computers were large, intimidating pieces of hardware that merely replaced slide rules for engineers and mathematicians. They filled entire rooms. Few people would have considered using one for personal or family applications. This small group of Apple Computer pirates, however, designed and developed the Macintosh computer—a fun, approachable, all-in-one kind of machine. It was the first to incorporate a mouse, icons (pictures) on a screen, and software that could actually paint a picture (Mac-Paint) on what formerly had been only a computational device. The team's endeavors were so successful (as was the rest of Apple's business) that the entire organization adopted the team culture and came to look like Profile 2 in Figure 3.5—a highly cohesive clan. Employees wore Apple logos on their clothes, had Apple bumper stickers on their cars, and spoke warmly of the "Apple family."

The enormous success of the company led it toward a third kind of culture, however. With hundreds of thousands of computers being sold, distribution channels expanding worldwide, and the emergence of a large array of highly competitive rivals (including IBM, Compaq, and Wang), the freewheeling clan faced a need for controls and standard procedures. Policies and regulations were needed; in other words, a hierarchy orientation had to be developed (Profile 3 in Figure 3.5). Jobs, Apple's CEO, was the quintessential innovator and team leader, perfectly comfortable in an organization dominated by adhocracy and clan cultures. He was not an efficiency expert and administrator and not inclined to manage a hierarchy. John Scully from PepsiCo was hired, therefore, to manage the shift to stability and control. Predictably, this shift created such a crisis in the organization—with the clan and adhocracy orientations being supplanted by a hierarchy orientation—that founder Jobs was actually ousted from the company. A new set of values and priorities reflected in a new culture made Jobs's orientation out of sync with current demands. The shift to a hierarchy culture generally produces a sense of apprehension, of abandoning core values, of replacing family feelings with rules and policies. Scully was a master efficiency and marketing expert, however, and his skills matched more closely the shifting culture of Apple as its growth produced a new cultural orientation.

As Apple developed into a large, mature organization under Scully, the culture shifted again to a fourth stage, Profile 4 in Figure 3.5. It ceased to be the agile, innovative company that characterized the young group of renegades in its early life but instead was an outstanding example of efficiency and marketing savvy. In many organizations, this profile becomes the norm, with the clan and adhocracy cultures being minimized and the hierarchy and market cultures being emphasized. Many management consultants and leadership gurus therefore spend a great deal of energy assisting companies in developing the capability to reinstitute clan- and adhocracy-like attributes so that they can be more balanced organizations. It is not that all four types of cultures must be emphasized equally. Rather, it is that the organization must develop the capability to shift emphases when the demands of the competitive environment require it.

One reason for the performance difficulties of Apple is the continued emphasis in the company's culture on the bottom two quadrants in Figure 3.5. In an industry faced in the late 1990s with the need to innovate constantly with very rapid cycle times, the continued cultural dominance by the bottom two quadrants, instead of a shift back up to the adhocracy quadrant, seems to have had significant negative effects on Apple's performance as a company until the development of the innovative iPod.

Culture Change in a Mature Organization

Culture change also occurs in large, mature organizations, but in a less predictable pattern. Culture change in these organizations must generally be managed consciously. One example of this kind of managed culture change was a midsize financial services company known as Meridian Bancorp (acquired by CoreStates Financial in 1996). As the firm grew from a $5 billion to a $15 billion company, the company's culture changed in response to new environmental and competitive pressures. This pattern of culture change was less standard, however, than that occurring in new, young companies.

The banking industry has traditionally been dominated by companies characterized as clan- and hierarchy-type organizations—highly regulated and controlled, tightly integrated, with multiple hierarchical levels and an old-boy network. Profile 1 in Figure 3.6

Figure 3.6 Culture Change in a Mature Organization

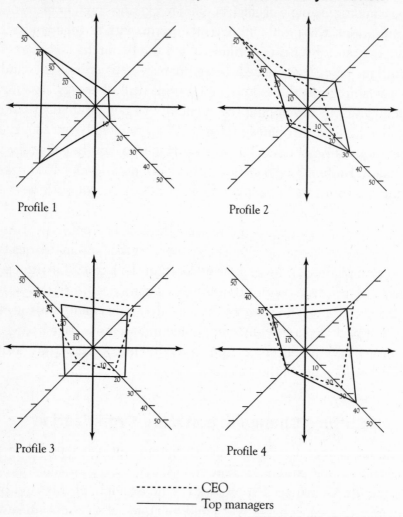

Profile 1

Profile 2

Profile 3

Profile 4

---------- CEO
———————— Top managers

characterizes the stereotypical banking culture. In the mid-1980s, the CEO at Meridian Bancorp and his top administrative team completed the OCAI. Profile 2 in Figure 3.6 provides a summary of the culture profile produced by these top officers, with the CEO's profile contrasted to those of his direct reports. It is clear that the cultural perspectives of this top management team were not compatible. The company had been founded on the tradition of a rural-bank, clan-type culture. Meridian's growth, however, which was primarily through acquisitions and mergers, led it into a more competitive, regional-focused environment. Whereas the president felt that the organization was still dominated by the traditional clan culture, his senior management team clearly felt the pressures of the increased competition.

Five years later, after continued expansion, the culture of the company had changed markedly to reflect the emergence of a more competitive, diversified financial services company. Many of the top management team members had been replaced, and as illustrated by Profile 3 in Figure 3.6, more congruence of perspective had developed. Meridian had begun to put more emphasis on the adhocracy culture, and the president's cultural perspective more nearly reflected those of his direct reports.

Thereafter, with additional changes in the top management team, escalating pressure from Wall Street to reduce expenses and to become more efficient, and continued escalation in competitive pressures, Meridian's culture made yet another shift. The company continued to value a cohesive, clan-type culture as well as a rational, hierarchy-type culture. But when the top management team completed the OCAI again, what dominated the values and perspectives in the organization was an emphasis on competitiveness and producing results (market culture) as well as new product development and innovation (adhocracy culture). Profile 4 in Figure 3.6 shows that that culture profile was almost the mirror image of the traditional banking culture that characterized most banking organizations prior to the mid-1980s. It also demonstrates the emergence of a congruent set of values, definitions, and perspectives among the top management team as they consciously managed the process of culture change in their company.

Summary

We have explained in some detail the development of the Competing Values Framework and its applicability to various aspects of organizations. Our intent is to illustrate how comprehensive the framework can be in organizing and highlighting the congruence of various aspects of managerial and organizational behavior. Our own research indicates that matches between the dominant culture of the organization and its leadership styles, management roles, human resource management, quality management, and effectiveness criteria contribute to higher levels of performance than mismatches do. Mismatches, of course, may create enough discomfort in the system to motivate changes, so they may serve a useful purpose for short periods of time. For the most part, however, the congruence of these various elements in organizations is a prerequisite to high performance, and the framework we have introduced here is useful as a guide for enhancing organizational effectiveness as well as for facilitating culture change.

Note

1. Joanne Martin (1992) at Stanford University, one of the best analysts and investigators of the concept of organizational culture, differentiated among three perspectives or approaches to culture. One perspective—the *integration* perspective—assumes that culture is what people share or serves as the glue that holds them together. Consensus about what culture exists in an organization can be detected. A second perspective—the *differentiation* perspective—assumes that culture is manifested by differences among subunits and that an organization's culture is fraught with conflicts of interest. Consensus about what common culture exists is fiction. A third perspective—the *fragmentation* perspective—assumes that culture is ambiguous and unknowable and that it describes not an attribute of an organization but the inherent nature of the organization itself. Individuals shift cultures frequently within an organization, and no one culture can be identified. Martin argued that each perspective has legitimacy and must be acknowledged as individuals study or try to manage culture.

    Although we agree with her assessment that elements of all three perspectives are present in organizations, the power of culture from our point of view lies in its ability to bring people together, to overcome the fragmentation and ambiguity that characterize the external environment, and to lead organizations toward extraordinary success when their competitors struggle. That is, this book is biased toward the *integration* approach to culture because it is in the integration perspective that culture derives its power. Culture is a competitive advantage in organizations mainly to the extent to which it is a common, consensual, integrated set of perceptions, memories, values, attitudes, and definitions. Moreover, it is our experience after working with a large number of organizations ranging from multinational conglomerates to small, entrepreneurial start-up firms, as well as being consistent with empirical evidence (reported in Appendix A), that managers can and do reach consensus about what the organization's culture is like, what approaches can be implemented to change it, and how the organization can become different as a result.

On the other hand, the approach to culture change described in this book relies on some of the assumptions of the differentiation and fragmentation approaches in that it acknowledges that ambiguous and unmanageable aspects of the organization always exist. The steps we describe in Chapter Five for managing the culture change process provide a tool for addressing those aspects of organizational culture.

4

CONSTRUCTING AN ORGANIZATIONAL CULTURE PROFILE

Near the end of his long and illustrious career, the renowned statistician John W. Tukey wrote *Exploratory Data Analysis* (1977). What is interesting about the book is that Tukey, the developer of the most frequently used statistical tests for assessing significant differences among sets of numbers, argued that insight and understanding are best created not by submitting data to statistical tests but by creating pictures of the data. He contended that the most effective way to interpret numbers is to plot them, draw pictures with them, chart them, or graph them. The pictures give people a better sense of what the numbers mean than a statistical test or a sophisticated mathematical technique. It is possible to see more relationships, do more comparisons, and identify more interesting patterns by analyzing images and representations than by simply looking at the results of numerical analyses.

Because our experience is similar to Tukey's, we encourage you to construct a picture of your organizational culture data. The purpose of this chapter is to help you draw cultural profiles that will highlight attributes of your organization's culture that may not be obvious without the pictures.

Plotting a Profile

The OCAI focuses on some core attributes of an organization that reflect its culture. Your ratings of these core attributes in Chapter Two produced an indication of the types of culture that are dominant in your organization. In other words, your responses on the six items helped highlight aspects of your organization's culture that identify its general culture type. To construct your own organizational culture profile, use the scores you computed in Figure 2.2 in Chapter Two. That is, you computed an average score for each alternative—A, B, C, and D—for the "Now" and the "Preferred" columns.

To construct an organizational culture profile, follow these three steps:

1. Consider first the "Now" column numbers. Plot the average scores for each alternative (A, B, C, and D) on the organizational culture profile form in Figure 4.1. The A alternative score represents the *clan* culture. Plot that number on the diagonal line extending upward in the top left quadrant on the form. The B alternative represents the *adhocracy* culture. Plot that number on the diagonal line extending upward in the upper right quadrant on the form. The C alternative represents the *market* culture. Plot that number on the diagonal line extending downward in the bottom right quadrant on the form. The D alternative represents the *hierarchy* culture. Plot that number on the diagonal line extending downward in the bottom left quadrant on the form.

2. Connect the points in each quadrant to form a four-sided figure. You will have produced some sort of kitelike shape. This profile creates a picture of your organization's culture as it exists right now. Such a picture is more useful for diagnostic purposes than the set of numbers produced in Chapter Two by themselves because it allows you to visualize your culture. You can see the more and less dominant aspects of the organization's culture.

3. Now plot the scores from the "Preferred" column on the same form. This time connect the points using a dotted line (or a different color) so as to distinguish your preferred culture from your current culture. Having both plots on the same form allows you to compare the extent to which the current culture matches the preferred culture and to identify where cultural change might be in order.

Figure 4.1 now reflects your organization's overall current and preferred culture. This is the combination of each of the separate core organizational attributes that reflect its culture.

It may also be informative to plot the scores for each of the individual questions or attributes of culture contained in the items in the OCAI. This permits you to determine the extent to which each cultural attribute reflects the same dominant culture type (that is, the extent to which your cultural plots are congruent). It also allows you to determine the extent to which the current culture matches (is congruent with) the preferred culture.

Figure 4.2 allows you to plot each of the six questions individually. To use Figure 4.2, follow these steps:

1. Look back at your "Now" column ratings on the OCAI in Chapter Two. Plot the scores from item 1 (Organizational Characteristics) on the form with the same label. Now plot the scores from item 2 (Organizational Leadership) on the figure with the same label. Do the same thing for each of the six questions on the appropriate form in Figure 4.2. Connect each of the points with a solid line so that a kitelike figure is produced on each form.

2. Now look back at your "Preferred" column ratings. Plot these ratings on the appropriate forms in Figure 4.2. Use a dotted line (or a different color) to connect the points so as to distinguish them from your "Now" ratings.

Examples of six illustrative organizational culture profiles are presented in Figure 4.3. These plots are not intended to be stereotypical or ideal; they just represent six randomly selected organizations, each of which has a slightly different organizational culture profile. We provide these different examples merely to illustrate the wide variety of culture profiles that organizations can develop. For example, the high-tech manufacturer, a maker of metering and measuring devices, is dominated by the adhocracy quadrant. Its survival depends on the rapid and constant innovation of new products and services for a hyperturbulent environment. The fast-growing bancorp is

Figure 4.1 Organizational Culture Profile

The Clan Culture

A very friendly place to work where people share a lot of themselves. It is like an extended family. The leaders, or head of the organization, are considered to be mentors and, maybe even, parent figures. The organization is held together by loyalty or tradition. Commitment is high. The organization emphasizes the long-term benefit of human resource development and attaches great importance to cohesion and morale. Success is defined in terms of sensitivity to customers and concern for people. The organization places a premium on teamwork, participation, and consensus.

The Adhocracy Culture

A dynamic, entrepreneurial, and creative place to work. People stick their necks out and take risks. The leaders are considered to be innovators and risk takers. The glue that holds the organization together is commitment to experimentation and innovation. The emphasis is on being on the leading edge. The organization's long-term emphasis is on growth and acquiring new resources. Success means gaining unique and new products or services. Being a product or service leader is important. The organization encourages individual initiative and freedom.

The Hierarchy Culture

A very formalized and structured place to work. Procedures govern what people do. The leaders pride themselves on being good coordinators and organizers, who are efficiency-minded. Maintaining a smooth-running organization is most critical. Formal rules and policies hold the organization together. The long-term concern is on stability and performance with efficient, smooth operations. Success is defined in terms of dependable delivery, smooth scheduling, and low cost. The management of employees is concerned with secure employment and predictability.

The Market Culture

A results-oriented organization. The major concern is getting the job done. People are competitive and goal-oriented. The leaders are hard drivers, producers, and competitors. They are tough and demanding. The glue that holds the organization together is an emphasis on winning. Reputation and success are common concerns. The long-term focus is on competitive actions and achievement of measurable goals and targets. Success is defined in terms of market share and penetration. Competitive pricing and market leadership are important. The organizational style is hard-driving competitiveness.

Figure 4.1 Organizational Culture Profile, Cont'd.

The Clan Culture

An organization that focuses on internal maintenance with flexibility, concern for people, and sensitivity to customers.

The Adhocracy Culture

An organization that focuses on external positioning with a high degree of flexibility and individuality.

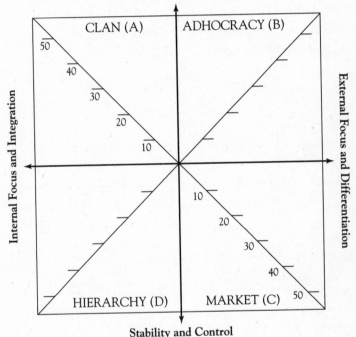

The Hierarchy Culture

An organization that focuses on internal maintenance with a need for stability and control.

The Market Culture

An organization that focuses on external positioning with a need for stability and control.

Figure 4.2 Profiles for Individual Items on the OCAI

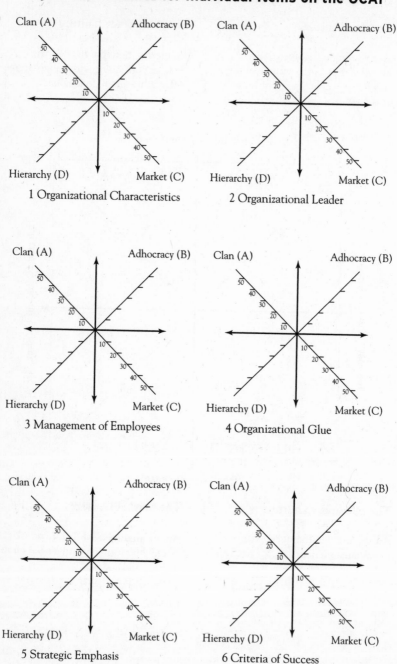

unusual in that its culture emphasizes the right side of the profile—adhocracy and market—similar to the Meridian example. Most banks have a mirror image of that profile. The standardized parts producer is dominated by a hierarchy culture, with the adhocracy culture being second most dominant. This firm produces millions of standardized parts annually and distributes them to the auto and aerospace industries. The multinational manufacturer, which produces and distributes products in more than fifty countries, clearly emphasizes the bottom two culture types, market and hierarchy. It operates in a highly competitive industry dominated by large manufacturers headquartered in at least a dozen countries. The U.S. federal government agency fits the stereotype of an efficient, stable, controlled system, dominated by the hierarchy quadrant. No surprises there. The data systems firm is one of the few organizations we have seen that has a close-to-zero score in the adhocracy culture. Parenthetically, this firm was purchased by another, larger firm to help stimulate the parent company in its development of new products and creation of innovations. Predictably, a great deal of conflict, discomfort, and disillusionment occurred for the first several months after the merger because this firm's culture was so incompatible with expectations in the parent firm. A diagnosis of culture type using the OCAI helped resolve some of the problems of culture incompatibility and mismatched expectations, and it helped stimulate a needed culture change process.

Interpreting the Culture Profiles

Having drawn a picture of your overall culture profile as well as the profiles of each of the six culture attributes, you can now interpret these profiles from several different perspectives. At least six comparison standards are available: (1) the *type* of culture that dominates your organization, (2) *discrepancies* between your current and your preferred future culture, (3) the *strength* of the culture type that dominates your organization, (4) the *congruence* of the culture profiles generated on different attributes and by different individuals in your

Figure 4.3 Culture Profiles for Six Organizations

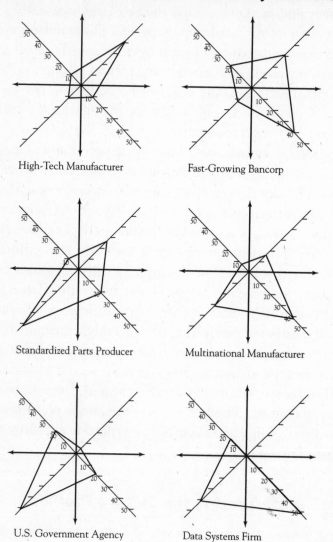

High-Tech Manufacturer   Fast-Growing Bancorp

Standardized Parts Producer   Multinational Manufacturer

U.S. Government Agency   Data Systems Firm

organization, (5) a *comparison* of your organization's culture profile with the average culture profiles of almost one thousand organizations as rated by approximately fourteen thousand of their managers, and (6) *trends* we have noticed in more than two decades of work with this culture instrument.

Type

Refer to your overall culture plot on the Organizational Cultural Profile (Figure 4.1). The quadrant in which scores are the highest indicates the culture that tends to be emphasized most in your organization. It identifies the basic assumptions, styles, and values that predominate. One reason it is useful to know your organization's culture type is because organizational success depends on the extent to which your organization's culture matches the demands of the competitive environment. A firm with a strong clan culture and a weak market culture that is operating in a fiercely competitive, highly aggressive industry may find it very difficult to survive because of a mismatch between culture and environment. Organizational cultures need to have some compatibility with the demands of their environments. In addition, as you consider your own long-term future in your organization, this culture profile will be useful for identifying what kinds of leadership attributes are most valued, what behaviors are most likely to be recognized and rewarded, and what kinds of management styles are preferred. In addition to deciding whether the culture is appropriate for your industry environment, therefore, you may also want to determine the extent to which the culture is compatible with your own long-term goals, style, and inclinations.

Discrepancies

Another important source of information is the discrepancies between your current organizational culture and what you prefer it to be. By observing the areas of greatest discrepancy between the preferred future culture and the current culture on the profiles in Figures 4.1 and 4.2, a road map for change can be determined. Look for the widest differences in what is preferred versus what is current. Be especially sensitive to differences of more than ten points. Consider what needs to be changed in order to close the gaps. In Chapter Five, we help you identify systematically what should be increased, what should be decreased, and what should remain the same to close these discrepancy gaps. Of course, you will not want to abandon aspects of culture types that are important even though they may not be dominant. Ultimately, discrepancy data may be the most powerful of all the data provided by your culture profile if your agenda is to initiate change.

Strength

The strength of your culture is determined by the number of points awarded to a specific culture type. The higher the score, the stronger or more dominant is that particular culture. Research has revealed that strong cultures are associated with homogeneity of effort, clear focus, and higher performance in environments where unity and common vision are required. Firms such as IBM, Procter & Gamble, Johnson & Johnson, and Apple have strong cultures. The extent to which your organization needs a strong dominant culture as opposed to a balanced or eclectic culture is a matter of individual circumstance and environment. The nature of the challenges your firm faces is likely to be the determining factor. Some organizations, for example, face circumstances where survival depends on flexibility, innovation, creativity, and entrepreneurship. Coordination and control are much less influential in determining successful performance. A strong adhocracy culture may be most appropriate. An example of such a firm is Intel, maker of integrated circuits in computers. Other organizations may require a more balanced culture where similar emphasis is required on each of the four culture types. No culture type may be strong in such a firm. Ford Motor Company, a firm that has led the world in cutting-edge design while at the same time manufacturing the world's largest-selling car (the Taurus), is sometimes known as a finance company but is being led by a true "car guy" who can service his own vehicle. None of the culture quadrants dominates in this firm. The point is that no ideal culture plot exists. Each organization must determine for itself the degree of cultural strength required to be successful in its environment.

Congruence

Cultural congruence means that various aspects of an organization's culture are aligned. That is, the same culture types are emphasized in various parts of the organization. For example, in a congruent culture, the strategy, leadership style, reward system, approach to managing employees, and dominant characteristics all tend to emphasize the same set of cultural values. In such an organization, each of the individual plots in Figure 4.2 would look similar. By contrast, an organization with an incongruent culture would have profiles in Figure 4.2 with different shapes. Each attribute would emphasize different culture types and show no particular pattern of similarity. Our own and others' research has found that congruent cultures, although not a prerequisite for success, are more typical of high-performing organizations than incongruent cultures. Having all aspects of the organization clear about and focused on the same values and sharing the same assumptions simply eliminates many of the complications, disconnects, and obstacles that can get in the way of effective performance.

The presence of cultural incongruence in organizations often stimulates an awareness of a need for change. It creates enough discomfort in the organization that members often complain about the ambiguity, lack of integration, or absence of fit they experience, or they bemoan the hypocrisy that they observe when organizational behaviors seem to be incompatible with what they perceive to be the espoused values. Of course, hypocrisy is not always a product of cultural incongruence, but it is often one of the major symptoms that incongruence exists in a culture. Cultural incongruence, in other words, often leads to differences in perspectives, differences in goals, and differences in strategies within the organization. These in turn sap the energy and the focus of organizational members. Temporary incongruence may be functional in that it can highlight aspects of the organization that are uncomfortable, or it can uncover previously unacknowledged aspects of the culture that are dysfunctional. Increased motivation for change in the culture may be a desirable result. In the long run, however, incongruence inhibits the organization's ability to perform at the highest levels of effectiveness.

In considering cultural congruence, it is important to be sensitive to the unit of analysis under examination. For example, if individuals from different parts of the organization are rating their own subunit, very different culture profiles may be produced in different subunits. This does not mean that the organization does not have a congruent culture. One subunit, say, the consumer products division, may have a very congruent culture that is quite different from that of, say, the information systems division. Congruency of culture and its association with high performance is more likely to be connected to unit performance than to the overall performance of a large, complex corporation. Overall organizational ratings in such cases may not be as accurate as subunit ratings, although they may highlight the common or shared cultural emphases.

In interpreting your organization's cultural congruence, therefore, look at the individual plots on Figure 4.2. To what extent are the shapes of the plots the same? Look for discrepancies in the culture types that predominate. Are any of the plots emphasizing cultures that are on the diagonal from one another, that is, cultures that are contradictory? This kind of discrepancy is more incongruent than when adjacent quadrants predominate. Look for discrepancies of more than ten points. When discrepancies do exist, they may indicate a lack of focus, that the culture is unclear to respondents, or that the complexity of the environment requires multiple emphases in different areas of the organization.

Comparisons

In our own research, we have surveyed more than eighty thousand managers representing well over three thousand organizations. One standard against which to compare your own organization's culture is to compare it to the "average" organization. Figure 4.4 presents a profile of the average culture plot of the organizations in our database. Figure 4.5 shows the average profile for each item on the OCAI for these organizations, and average profiles for different industry groups are provided in Figure 4.6. The categorization scheme is based on standard industrial codes (codes that cluster similar organizational types together). These figures simply illustrate the cultural differences that exist among different organizational types.

Figure 4.4 Average Culture Plot for More Than One Thousand Organizations

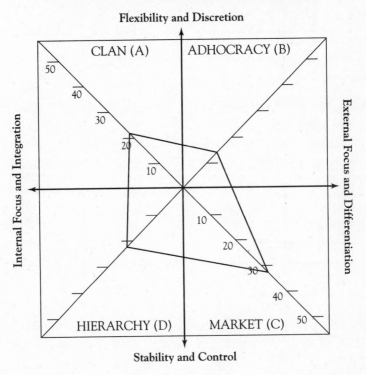

Figure 4.5 Average Profile for Each Item on the OCAI

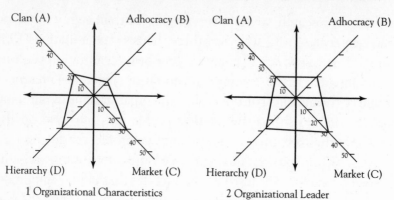

1 Organizational Characteristics

2 Organizational Leader

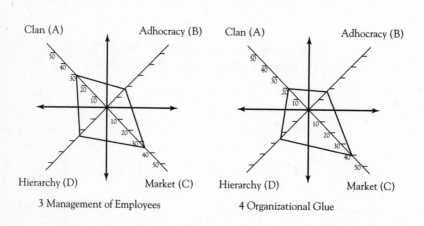

3 Management of Employees

4 Organizational Glue

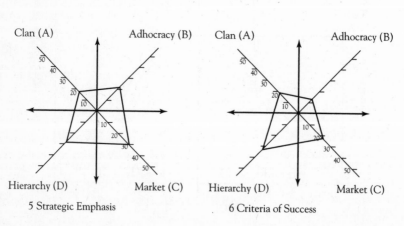

5 Strategic Emphasis

6 Criteria of Success

Figure 4.6 Average Culture Profile
for Various Industry Groups

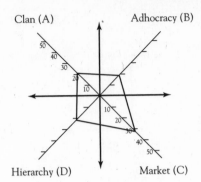

Agriculture, Forestry, Fishing
N=72

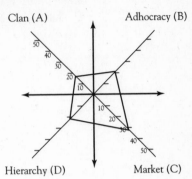

Nonclassifiable
N=9

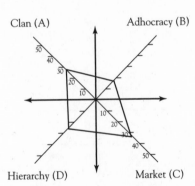

Finance, Insurance, Real Estate
N=172

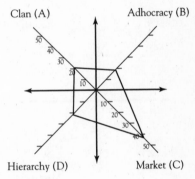

Manufacturing
N=38

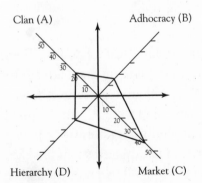

Mining
N=21

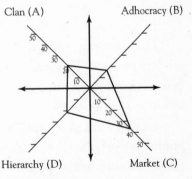

Construction
N=9

Figure 4.6 Average Culture Profile for Various Industry Groups, Cont'd.

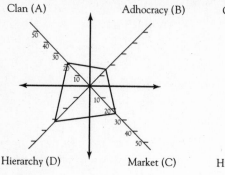

Public Administration
N=43

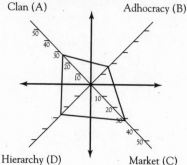

Services
N=7

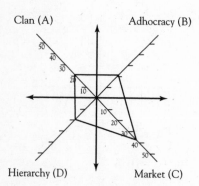

Retail and Wholesale Trade
N=44

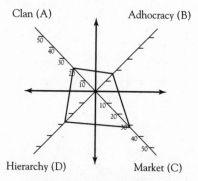

Transportation, Communications,
Electric, Gas, and Sanitary
N=127

These average plots do not represent an ideal, of course. They are just averages. Performance varies widely among these firms. The best-performing organizations in the world are represented as well as some organizations that aren't doing very well. A large number of industries are also represented, as well as organizations in the public and private sectors. A majority of the organizations are U.S. firms, but substantial numbers of firms from all five continents are also in the data set. It may be interesting for you to see if your own culture plot varies widely from the average organizational culture plot in your industry. If it does (or if it does not), ask yourself questions such as these: Does our culture adequately map our environmental demands? What changes are needed to bring our culture into alignment with our environmental demands? Are we emphasizing what our customers expect? In what areas are we underdeveloped? In what areas might we be overdeveloped or placing undue emphasis? In what areas do we have a unique advantage? Where does our core competency lie? Comparing your own organization's profile with your industry's profile and with the average industry profiles for each OCAI item may help stimulate additional insights for changing your culture in a way that enhances organizational effectiveness. Having a culture profile different from your industry's, for example, may mean that your organization has a unique competitive advantage, or it may mean that a mismatch is present with the demands of the industry's environment.

Trends

In our observation of more than one thousand organizations, several trends have emerged that seem to be typical. These trends may not represent your organization at all, but they are offered to help provide additional understanding of your culture profiles.

1. Top managers tend to have higher clan scores. They rate the culture of the organization as more clan-focused than managers at lower levels of the hierarchy.

2. Adhocracy scores are generally rated the lowest, as you can tell from Figures 4.4 and 4.5. Not only is the average adhocracy score slightly lower than the others, but fewer firms are dominated by the adhocracy culture than are dominated by each of the other three culture types.

3. Over time, companies tend to gravitate toward an emphasis on the hierarchy and market culture types. Once their culture profiles become dominated by those lower two quadrants, it seems to be difficult for them to emphasize the upper two quadrants. It's almost as if gravity takes over. The lower quadrants have a tendency

to remain dominant the longest. It takes a great deal of effort and leadership to make the change to a clan or adhocracy culture.

4. Several management consultants and authors have equated "leadership" with the cultures associated with the top two quadrants and "management" with the cultures in the bottom two quadrants. It has become quite popular, for example, for writers and commentators to advocate leadership and not management; that is, they emphasize teamwork, innovation, and change (clan and adhocracy) instead of maintaining stability, productivity, and the status quo (hierarchy and market). We do not happen to agree with this common distinction between leadership and management. Our research suggests that it takes both leadership and management to strengthen, maintain, change, or create a culture in any of the quadrants. Leaders who are not managers are bound to fail, just as managers who are not leaders are bound to fail. Change without stability is chaos. Innovation without productivity is pie in the sky. The distinction is not very useful, therefore, because both leadership and management are needed for organizational effectiveness. This is another important insight highlighted by the Competing Values Framework of culture. All four culture types (and the management competencies that accompany them) are valuable and necessary. None is better or worse than the others.

5. Paradoxes often exist in cultural profiles. It is not unusual to see cigar-shaped profiles, for example. It need not be the case that an organization must be dominated by one side of the organization profile form or the other or that it emphasizes the top or the bottom of the profile. Many high-performing organizations simultaneously emphasize the clan culture along with the market culture or the hierarchy culture along with the adhocracy culture. This may be a sign of strength as much as a sign of weakness. For example, in some of our own research (Cameron, 1986), we found that organizational effectiveness in institutions of higher education was highest in organizations that emphasized innovation and change (adhocracy) and at the same time stability and control (hierarchy). We also found that effective organizations were supportive of and developed

their employees (clan) but also demanded output and achievement from them (market). We concluded in that study, in other words, that effective organizations are able to behave in flexible and sometimes contradictory ways. They can encourage hard-driving productivity and accomplishment, yet also empower employees and maintain a fun, informal climate.

Summary

Our point in this chapter was to briefly explain ways to analyze your organizational culture profile. Our intent, throughout the book, is to help you understand the strengths and potential for change in your own organization's culture. Understanding how your organization is the same as and different from other similar organizations, how its different elements are aligned with one another, and in what ways change might be initiated are all important outcomes from this brief analysis of profiles.

In the next chapter, we describe a procedure for systematically designing a culture change process. We use examples from a real organizational culture change effort to illustrate this procedure.

5

USING THE FRAMEWORK TO DIAGNOSE AND CHANGE ORGANIZATIONAL CULTURE

The usefulness of this framework is that it serves as a way to diagnose and initiate change in the underlying organizational culture that organizations develop as they progress through their life cycles and as they cope with the pressures of their external environments. Each organizational culture profile reflects underlying attributes, including the management style, strategic plans, climate, reward system, means of bonding, leadership, and basic values of the organization. Changing the culture, then, requires that these various elements of culture be identified and altered. This identification and alternative-generation task is a key challenge faced by individuals interested in initiating culture change.

In this chapter, we provide a useful methodology for identifying what needs to change in an organization's culture and for developing a strategy to initiate change in key elements. The methodology relies on a process of dialogue among individuals charged with initiating and managing the change. This usually involves managers near the top of the organization, but it may involve organization members at all levels.

Because the culture of most organizations is invisible and taken for granted, most organization members have a difficult time identifying or describing it, let alone consciously changing it. This is where the OCAI can be especially useful. The instrument helps uncover, or bring to the surface, aspects of the organization's culture that might otherwise not be identifiable or articulated by organization members. The OCAI allows a manager or a potential change agent to say to organization members, "Here is a tool we can use to identify key characteristics of our culture. It focuses on six elements that reflect who we are and how we approach organizational challenges. This instrument allows us to measure where our organization is and where we want to be. We can use the OCAI as part of a systematic process to specify what the measures of culture mean in terms of action. It will help us formulate an action agenda."

As you will see in this chapter, the process of culture change can be used by novices or by experienced change agents. In fact, the instrument and methodology have already been used by scores of consulting firms and change agents worldwide to initiate the culture change process. However, we have written the book in order that managers untrained as change agents can also use the methodology to initiate their own change initiatives. In Appendix B, we provide some helpful suggestions for initiating culture changes in various areas of an organization. Those suggestions supplement the methodology described in this chapter, and they are provided to help managers who are inexperienced in managing a culture change process do so effectively. More experienced change agents, on the other hand, may use the OCAI and this methodology to address deep obstacles to culture change and to facilitate major corporate transformations. Whereas the methodology described is linear and stepwise, a large number of variations in this process may be used to lead organization members through a culture change initiative.

One way to illustrate the usefulness of this methodology is to describe a well-known organization that relied on the OCAI diagnosis procedure to initiate culture change. This organization became convinced that improving organizational effectiveness was predicated on a significant program of cultural change (see Hooijberg and Petrock, 1993). After describing the case study, we present a six-step methodology for employing the OCAI. Then we provide two more case studies illustrating some variations on the OCAI methodology that address deep-change issues.

Planning for Culture Change: An Example

In an effort to become more competitive, the top management team of a well-known company decided to initiate significant organizational change. The organization is a large multinational business that manufactures circuit boards for the microelectronics industry. The environment is fast-paced, quick-to-change, and extremely competitive. The introduction of self-managing work teams was a key element identified by top managers to achieve desired organizational change. These managers were concerned, however, that initiating self-management might not survive the command-and-control work culture that had developed in the organization and had become institutionalized over the previous twenty years.

The methodology for diagnosing and initiating a culture change proceeded through a series of steps. Top management first convened a leadership team consisting of about twenty-five representatives from management, employees, and the union. Their charge was to reach agreement on the type of organizational culture needed to meet the competitive demands of the future and to sustain participative management processes such as self-managing work teams. The team members each completed the OCAI in order to diagnose the current organization's culture. They then were divided into six groups each containing representatives from management, employees, and the union. Each group reached consensus on ratings of the dimensions of culture being assessed. Each of the six group culture plots were averaged together to form an overall culture plot for the organization. The solid line in Figure 5.1 shows the final plot that emerged from this process.

The next task was to reach consensus on the preferred or future culture profile for the organization. This was accomplished by having each team member complete the OCAI again according to how he or she thought the culture should be in the future to ensure successful performance. The groups reached consensus on a preferred future culture and then reached consensus as an entire team on the preferred organizational culture profile. The dotted line in Figure 5.1

Figure 5.1 Profile of One Organization's Current and Preferred Cultures

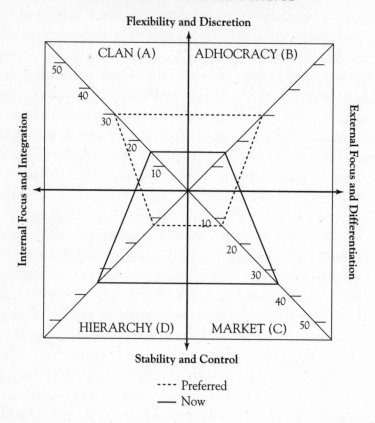

shows the end product of this process—a profile of the organization's current culture compared to the preferred future culture. Based on the differences between the current and preferred profiles, the leadership team determined which aspects of the organization's culture to emphasize more, which to emphasize less, and which to emphasize the same amount. From Figure 5.1 it is evident that the organization wanted to emphasize the clan and adhocracy quadrants more and the hierarchy and market quadrants less. Significant potential inhibitors to self-management existed because the culture did not emphasize the clan culture type enough.

Based on the discrepancies between the current and ideal culture profiles, the teams then reached consensus on what it means and what it does not mean to increase and decrease emphasis in each quadrant. For example, to increase emphasis in the clan quadrant means that more support and employee involvement must be emphasized. It does not mean that people can do whatever they want or that they can stop working hard. This step is to remind team members of the trade-offs that must be kept in mind whenever culture change occurs. It also points out the necessity of not abandoning some cultural emphases even though they are not the current priority in the culture change strategy. Figure 5.2 illustrates the data generated in this step by the team.

Finally, the team identified specific activities that could be implemented in order that the clan and adhocracy cultures could be enhanced and the hierarchy and market cultures could be deemphasized. The company did not want to abandon the hierarchy and market cultures altogether, of course, nor did it want to go overboard and focus exclusively on the clan and adhocracy quadrants. Therefore, the teams identified what they wanted to do more of, less of, and the same amount of in each of the four culture types. Action plans for implementing the changes that were implied by these lists were formulated, and a strategy for changing the organization's culture was initiated.

The ultimate result of this cultural diagnosis activity was the successful implementation of a self-managing team approach to culture change, with minimal resistance and with a greater shared awareness of the underlying strengths and future direction of the firm. Without this initial cultural diagnosis, embedded organizational resistance emanating from an entrenched but outdated culture would have subverted any such changes.

Steps for Designing an Organizational Culture Change Process

Using this organization's experience as an example, we present a six-step process that should be followed when designing and

Figure 5.2 One Organization's "Means-Does Not Mean" Analysis

Clan Culture	Adhocracy Culture
☑ Increase ☐ Decrease ☐ Remain Same	☑ Increase ☐ Decrease ☐ Remain Same

Clan Culture

Means . . .

Survey and meet employee needs
Promote teamwork and participation
Support and recognize team players
Foster better morale through
  empowerment
Create higher levels of trust
Express more obvious concern for
  people
Provide chances for self-management

Does Not Mean . . .

Becoming undisciplined and overly
  permissive
Perpetuating cliques jockeying for
  power
One big "love-in"
Only fostering an internal focus
Not working hard and having high
  expectations
Forgetting about stretch goals—
  protecting underperformers
Freedom without responsibility

Adhocracy Culture

Means . . .

Put dynamism back into the business
Encourage and celebrate risk taking
Foster creative alternatives and
  innovation
Make change the rule, not the
  exception
Become a more forward-looking
  organization
Create bolder innovation programs
Clarify a vision of the future

Does Not Mean . . .

Running the business with reckless
  abandon
Disregarding customer requirements
Selfishness and self-aggrandizement
Missing goals
The latest of everything
Taking unnecessary and uninformed
  risks
Abandoning careful analysis and
  projections

Figure 5.2 One Organization's "Means-Does Not Mean" Analysis, Cont'd.

Hierarchy Culture	Market Culture
☐ Increase ☑ Decrease ☐ Remain Same	☐ Increase ☑ Decrease ☐ Remain Same

Hierarchy Culture	Market Culture
Means . . .	*Means . . .*
Eliminate useless rules and procedures Eliminate unneeded reports and paperwork Reduce corporate directives Eliminate micromanagement Remove unnecessary constraints Push decision making down	Slightly less centrality of measures and financial indicators Stop driving for numbers at all costs Focus on key goals Constantly motivate our people Adapt to human as well as market needs Remember that we still need to make money
Does Not Mean . . .	*Does Not Mean . . .*
Loss of logical structure Letting the inmates run the asylum with no guidance Elimination of accountability and measurement Elimination of production schedules Slack time schedules and responsiveness Taking advantage of the situation	Ignoring the competition Losing the spirit of winning and our will to be number one Missing stretch goals and targets Neglecting the customer Missing profit projections and budgets Stop looking at results

implementing an organizational culture change effort. The purpose of these six steps is to foster involvement and to minimize resistance to the culture change by those affected, to clarify for all concerned what the new cultural emphases will be, to identify what is to remain unaltered in the organization in the midst of change, and to generate specific action steps that can be initiated to create momentum toward culture change.

The six steps for initiating organizational culture change are as follows:

1. Reach consensus on the current culture.

2. Reach consensus on the desired future culture.

3. Determine what the changes will and will not mean.

4. Identify illustrative stories.

5. Develop a strategic action plan.

6. Develop an implementation plan.

Let us examine each step in order.

Step 1: Reach Consensus on the Current Culture

Identify a set of key individuals in the organization who have a perspective of the overall organizational culture. Be sure to involve people who will be engaged in implementing change initiatives and whose acceptance is necessary for ensuring a successful change effort. Each of these individuals should complete the OCAI. Make sure that each person is rating the same organization when completing the instrument. That is, make certain that some people are not rating, say, a division while others are rating the overall firm. It is important to make certain that the target of analysis is the same for all respondents. Have these individuals meet together to generate a consensual view of the current organizational culture. Do not average ratings. Rather, consider carefully the perspectives of individuals who may see the organization differently than others. If the number of people completing the instrument is large, divide them into subgroups and have each subgroup create an overall, consensual culture plot. Do not ignore any person's ratings, no matter how discrepant. It is especially important to discuss the factors that led each individual to rate the organization's culture as he or she did. This discussion, and the reaching of consensus, is usually the most fruitful part of the exercise because it builds understanding, opens lines of communication, and expands appreciation of others' points of view. Having every person complete the OCAI individually permits them to think deeply about how they view the organization's culture, encourages participation by everyone, and generates the maximum amount of information needed to construct an overall culture profile.

After each subgroup has reached consensus on a current organizational culture profile, representatives from each subgroup meet together to generate an overall, consensual organizational culture profile. In these consensus-building discussions, the team should address questions such as the following: On what basis did you give the ratings that you did? What organizational or managerial behaviors reflect your ratings? What is being ignored in our organization? What is most highly valued by members of our organization? How is the organization different now from the way it was in the past? What events reflect our organization's culture? What symbols and manifestations are present that accurately depict our culture?

Step 2: Reach Consensus on the Desired Future Culture

As a separate step, repeat the process in Step 1, this time focusing on the preferred or desired culture. Keep the discussion of current culture separate from the discussion of the preferred culture so that the two are not just reflections of one another. In order to create a preferred culture, discuss questions such as the following: What will our organization need to be like to be highly successful in the future? What demands will we face in the future environment? What trends should we be aware of? In what areas would we like to be at the leading edge? Where are we currently underdeveloped? What will our customers or competitors require of us in the future? If we were to dominate our industry, what would need to change in our organization?

Remember that everyone should be involved in these discussions. No one's point of view should be ignored. Make certain that individuals provide as much rationale and evidence as possible for their perspectives. Don't conduct the discussion on an ethereal or "blue-sky" basis, but ground the discussion on informed projections, specific examples, and verifiable data. Discussion of these issues should help produce a consensual preferred culture toward which the organization must move. Again, make certain that this consensus-building process is not short-circuited. For example, don't just average numbers together. The discussion itself is likely to be among the most valuable aspects of the entire process.

Step 3: Determine What the Changes Will and Will Not Mean

Plot the current and preferred culture profiles on the form in Figure 5.3, and highlight the discrepancies. The absence of large discrepancies does not mean that important changes are not needed. Small shifts may be as important as large transformational shifts. Moreover, it may be as difficult to make small changes in a particular type of culture as a large change. A small increase in emphasis in the adhocracy quadrant, for example, may require as much energy and effort as a large increase. On the plotting form, the area of incongruence between the current and preferred culture plots identifies the changes that should be concentrated on.

The most important part of this step is to now have individuals complete the form in Figure 5.4. Each person identifies what it means and what it does not mean to emphasize or deemphasize a certain culture type. Keep in mind that trying to move toward one particular type of culture does not mean that other culture types should be abandoned or ignored. It only means that special emphasis must be placed on certain elements if the culture change is going to be successful. Questions that should be addressed include the following: What are the attributes that we want to emphasize if we are to move toward the preferred quadrant? What characteristics should dominate our new culture? What attributes should be reduced or abandoned if we are to move away from a particular quadrant? Even though we will move away from a quadrant, what characteristics will be preserved? What continues to be important about this culture type even though we will begin to emphasize another culture type? What are the most important trade-offs? How will we recognize the new culture?

Now the team must reach consensus on the key factors listed in each section of Figure 5.4. That is, identify the core attributes and principles that describe what it means and what it doesn't mean to change emphases in specific culture types. Be prepared to explain this table to others in order to help them understand how the culture will change. The intent of this step, in other words, is to create a broad, consensual vision of what the desired future will be, what the critical elements of the organization will be, what will change and what won't change, and what will be preserved that is so valuable in the current organizational culture.

As a side note, our colleague Alan Wilkins (1989) identified the importance of building on what he termed corporate character in any organizational change effort. What this means, in brief, is capitalizing on the core competencies, the unique mission, and the special organizational identity that has been created over time. Corporate character is similar to family traditions or a national consciousness. Organizations don't want to abandon some aspects of what makes them unique, but they do want to alter other things. Identifying what change means and doesn't mean helps remind individuals that they must not abandon certain core competencies of the organization. Team members will want to preserve some elements of their organization at all costs, even though these attributes may reside in a quadrant that is being emphasized less than another.

Step 4: Identify Illustrative Stories

Organizational culture is best communicated and illustrated by stories (Martin, Feldman, Hatch, and Sitkin, 1983; Martin and Powers, 1983). That is, the key values, desired orientations, and behavioral principles that are to characterize the new organizational culture are usually more clearly communicated through stories than in any other way. It is rare to talk to someone at FedEx, for example, without hearing the story about the employee who rented a helicopter,

Figure 5.3 Form for Plotting the Organizational Culture Profile

The Clan Culture

A very friendly place to work where people share a lot of themselves. It is like an extended family. The leaders, or head of the organization, are considered to be mentors and, maybe even, parent figures. The organization is held together by loyalty or tradition. Commitment is high. The organization emphasizes the long-term benefit of human resource development and attaches great importance to cohesion and morale. Success is defined in terms of sensitivity to customers and concern for people. The organization places a premium on teamwork, participation, and consensus.

The Adhocracy Culture

A dynamic, entrepreneurial, and creative place to work. People stick their necks out and take risks. The leaders are considered to be innovators and risk takers. The glue that holds the organization together is commitment to experimentation and innovation. The emphasis is on being on the leading edge. The organization's long-term emphasis is on growth and acquiring new resources. Success means gaining unique and new products or services. Being a product or service leader is important. The organization encourages individual initiative and freedom.

The Hierarchy Culture

A very formalized and structured place to work. Procedures govern what people do. The leaders pride themselves on being good coordinators and organizers, who are efficiency-minded. Maintaining a smooth-running organization is most critical. Formal rules and policies hold the organization together. The long-term concern is on stability and performance with efficient, smooth operations. Success is defined in terms of dependable delivery, smooth scheduling, and low cost. The management of employees is concerned with secure employment and predictability.

The Market Culture

A results-oriented organization. The major concern is getting the job done. People are competitive and goal-oriented. The leaders are hard drivers, producers, and competitors. They are tough and demanding. The glue that holds the organization together is an emphasis on winning. Reputation and success are common concerns. The long-term focus is on competitive actions and achievement of measurable goals and targets. Success is defined in terms of market share and penetration. Competitive pricing and market leadership are important. The organizational style is hard-driving competitiveness.

Figure 5.3 Form for Plotting the Organizational Culture Profile, Cont'd.

The Clan Culture

An organization that focuses on internal maintenance with flexibility, concern for people, and sensitivity to customers.

The Adhocracy Culture

An organization that focuses on external positioning with a high degree of flexibility and individuality.

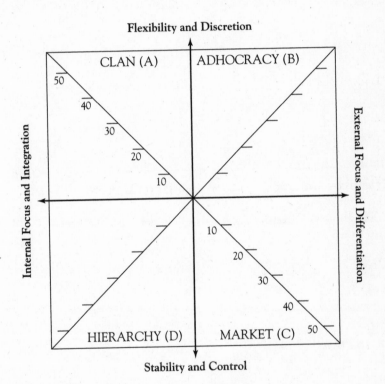

The Hierarchy Culture

An organization that focuses on internal maintenance with a need for stability and control.

The Market Culture

An organization that focuses on external positioning with a need for stability and control.

Figure 5.4 What Culture Change
Means and Does Not Mean

Clan Culture

☐ Increase   ☐ Decrease
☐ Remain Same

Means . . .

Does Not Mean . . .

Adhocracy Culture

☐ Increase   ☐ Decrease
☐ Remain Same

Means . . .

Does Not Mean . . .

Hierarchy Culture

☐ Increase   ☐ Decrease
☐ Remain Same

Means . . .

Does Not Mean . . .

Market Culture

☐ Increase   ☐ Decrease
☐ Remain Same

Means . . .

Does Not Mean . . .

flew to a mountaintop in a snowstorm, and fixed a transformer that had knocked out the phone system, illustrating the value of customer service and timeliness. A common story at Southwest Airlines describes the CEO working on the baggage line on holidays so that employees can take the day off, illustrating the value that customers are number two and employees are number one at Southwest and "positively outrageous service" applies first to fellow employees. The lessons that employees are to learn about appropriate behavior in the new culture are quickly and clearly communicated by telling and retelling stories that illustrate the desired values, attributes, and morals.

In this step, therefore, the team should identify two or three incidents or events that illustrate the key values they want to permeate the future organizational culture. These incidents or events should be associated with the organization itself so that members can identify with the values being illustrated. Actually tell the stories in the team discussions so that the group agrees they are powerful enough to convey the desired values and culture. Articulate clearly the lessons to be learned and the morals of the stories. These stories will serve the same functions as an exciting and clearly articulated vision of the future. They will be more powerful in communicating the new culture to others than any number of culture plots, lists of strategies, or motivational speeches by the CEO.

Step 5: Develop a Strategic Action Plan

Now that a shared understanding of what it means and doesn't mean to change the organization's culture has been developed, as well as what values are to be reinforced, the fifth step involves determining the specific actions to be taken to foster the desired change. The form in Figure 5.5 should be completed so that a few key actions are identified in each quadrant. As a team, reach consensus on what should be started, what should be stopped, and what should be continued in order for the culture change process to begin. This step requires, in other words, that the team identify actions and behaviors

Figure 5.5 Actions to Be Taken

Clan Culture	Adhocracy Culture
What should we do MORE of?	What should we do MORE of?
What should we START?	What should we START?
What should we STOP?	What should we STOP?
Hierarchy Culture	**Market Culture**
What should we do MORE of?	What should we do MORE of?
What should we START?	What should we START?
What should we STOP?	What should we STOP?

that will be undertaken as part of the culture change. As these action steps are formulated, keep in mind questions such as the following: What small things can be started or stopped? What wasteful, redundant, non-value-adding, or attention-deflecting activities need to be terminated? Where should we begin? What should be recognized and celebrated to build support for the change? What resources need to be garnered? What symbolic events can be initiated that signal the beginning of a new culture? What processes or systems should be redesigned? How can the new cultural values be communicated clearly? What metaphors can be used to reflect the new culture?

Of course, in order to make these change efforts effective, several important principles of organizational change must be kept in mind. The following suggestions do not constitute a comprehensive list, of course, but they do provide a helpful set of guidelines to consider as you determine what to start, stop, and continue.

- *Identify small wins.* Find something easy to change, change it, and celebrate it publicly. Then find a second thing that is easy to change, change it, and publicize it. Small successful steps create momentum in the desired direction and inhibit resistance. It is often not worth opposing small changes.

- *Generate social support.* Build coalitions of supporters for the change and empower them. Involve those affected by the changes. Listen to their perspectives, and help them feel understood, valued, and engaged.

- *Design follow-up and accountability.* Specify time frames for changes to be completed, design follow-up and reporting events, and develop mechanisms for ensuring that people follow through on commitments and assignments so that change really occurs. Don't let the change be open-ended. Set targets for incremental completions.

- *Provide information.* Share as much information as possible on a regular basis and as broadly as possible. In the absence of information, people create their own, so reduce rumors and ambiguity by opening lines of communication, providing factual information, providing personal feedback to those involved, and especially, celebrating successes publicly.

- *Measure.* Identify the criteria that will indicate successful culture change. Define a data gathering system and a time frame for assessing results. What gets measured gets attention, so make certain you measure the most critical and the most central factors. Since you can't measure everything, make sure you measure what counts.

- *Create readiness.* You can be sure that resistance to culture change will occur. This is because the basic values and way of life that people have become accustomed to are being changed. Creating readiness to change may be fostered by identifying the advantages of the future state, identifying the disadvantages of not changing, showing gaps between current performance and future required performance, providing needed resources to implement change, and rewarding behaviors compatible with the desired change.

- *Explain why.* When people know why the change is necessary, most of their resistance subsides. Moreover, research in communication suggests that people tend to explain why to people they care about and hold in high esteem. They tend to tell *what* to those they care less about or hold in low esteem. Explaining why therefore communicates both caring and esteem to those involved in the culture change process.

- *Hold a funeral.* Sometimes in order to make a case for a change, the past is criticized or denigrated. The problem is that most of us were part of the past, as we will be a part of the future. We often feel that criticism diminishes our efforts in the past. So consider holding a funeral. Funerals celebrate the past, but they make a transition to a future that will be different. The past wasn't bad; it is just different from the future.

- *Implement symbolic as well as substantive change.* Among the most important changes that accompanies culture change is a change in symbols. Identify symbols that signify a new future. These help people visualize something different, help change the mental interpretation systems of people as well as the organizational systems, and provide something for people to rally around.

- *Focus on processes.* For change to last, it must be reflected in the core processes in which the organization is engaged. This means that the process of selecting, appraising, and rewarding people must be changed to reflect the new culture. It means that the core business processes, such as designing, engineering, manufacturing, delivering, and servicing products, may need to be redesigned. Rearranging structures or reporting relationships will not contribute to long-term success by themselves. Process changes must occur.

Be sure that the list of action steps is not so long that it is impossible to implement. After each member of the team has developed his or her own list, identify the consensual points, the most powerful ones, and the ones that will have the most impact in the long run.

Step 6: Develop an Implementation Plan

The final step is to create an implementation plan, complete with timetables and short-term benchmarks, that will initiate the process of culture change. Specifically, identify the few key ways that the culture change process can unfold. Target the main themes that emerge from the activities in Steps 4 and 5. Decide on the four or five (at most) things that will receive the major portion of your attention and energy. Form teams or task forces and have each tackle one key theme or change target. Then personalize the culture change. Identify the behaviors and competencies that each team member will need to develop or improve to reflect the new culture. Chapter Six provides a specific method for personalizing the culture change process.

Of course, changing culture is a difficult and long-term effort. It will be necessary, over time, to address almost every aspect of the organization to ensure that it is aligned and reinforces the preferred culture. One way to remember the various aspects of the organization that need to be considered is to use a variation on the "Seven S" model first introduced by Waterman, Peters, and Phillips (1980): recognize that successful culture change may require a change in *structure* (the organization's architecture), *symbols* (the images that reinforce culture), *systems* (such as the production system, appraisal system, selection system, and quality system), *staff* (the selection and development of human resources), *strategy* (behavioral manifestations of the organization's vision), *style of leaders* (the attitudes and examples set by top leaders), and *skills of managers* (the competencies of individuals who must carry out the change processes). Alignment of these factors will be an important part of successful culture change.

This sixth step in the culture change process will most likely involve creating readiness for and overcoming resistance to change among your organization members. A communication and modeling strategy will need to be developed so that the new cultural values are exemplified by those leading the change. The system changes that must be made to reinforce the new culture—including selection, development, incentive, production, and distribution systems—will need to be identified. Mechanisms for helping organization members feel committed to the new preferred culture will need to be designed. The first steps to be taken need to be orchestrated. Questions such as the following may require specific answers: In what ways can employees become involved in fashioning and carrying out the change strategies? How can continuous communication of the new cultural values be ensured? What information needs to be shared and with whom? How will we know we are making progress in the change effort? What are the key indicators of successful change? What measurement system is needed?

Culture change will not occur without the involvement, commitment, and active support of organization members throughout the entire organization. One strategy to facilitate this process of commitment and support was used by Xerox Corporation when it faced a tremendous need for culture change. After its patent protection on the photocopying process ran out, Xerox found that its manufacturing costs were 30 percent higher than the retail price of Canon's copier. The quality of Xerox copiers was significantly lower than that of the competitive machines. Without dramatic change, Xerox would have gone out of business. One key to that process was a simple method outlined in Figure 5.6.

Organization members were organized into family groups, based primarily on hierarchical level. The top management group (Family Group 1) established and clearly articulated a vision for the future, identified the preferred culture, and learned some principles of organization and culture change. Then they were required to formulate action plans for themselves personally as well as for the group. The third step was to teach the principles to others, share

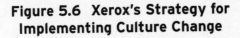

Figure 5.6 Xerox's Strategy for Implementing Culture Change

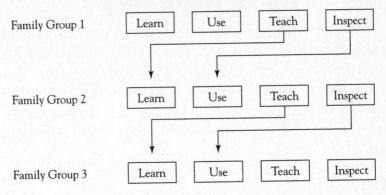

Group members are exposed to information four times:
1. When they learn the principles
2. When they use them
3. When they teach them
4. When they inspect someone else's application

the vision, and explain the rational for the new culture. The individuals they taught were those in the family group at the next lower level in the hierarchy. Fourth, the members of Family Group 1 were required to monitor or assess the effectiveness of the change efforts. They not only monitored their own actions but also served as outside auditors for the change plans of Family Group 2. This same process was repeated for Family Group 2, who targeted Family Group 3 as the focus of its teaching and assessments.

Consequently, the members of each family group were exposed to the new culture in four different ways and four times: when they learned about it, when they formulated action plans to try to achieve it, when they taught it to others, and when they assessed or measured it. Step 1, learning about it, helped clarify the key principles on which change was based. Step 2, formulating an action plan, made the culture change personal. It could not be delegated to someone else. Personal change was required. Step 3, teaching, helped clarify the preferred culture, created commitment to it by the teachers, and provided involvement for the entire organization. Step 4, monitoring, helped clarify the key criteria that indicated success.

We suggest that you follow a strategy similar to Xerox's in your own culture change efforts. Your change process will be more successful if you have a rational strategy for implementing the culture change, rather than just hoping that somehow things will be different in the future. After all, the axiom is true: If you do the things you've always done, you'll get the results you've always gotten.

Summary

Our intent in outlining these six steps for implementing culture change is to help ensure that the organization is clear from the outset about its current culture and why it needs to change. A common mistake in organizations desiring to improve is that they do not take the time to arrive at a common viewpoint among employees about where the organization is starting from and where it needs to go. Unsuccessful organizations often launch right into a new change program without considering the need to develop a consensual view of the current culture, the need to reach consensus of what change means and doesn't mean, and the specific changes that will be started, stopped, and continued. This six-step strategy will help you overcome these common obstacles to change and make the management of culture change more systematic.

Culture change at a deep level, of course, may require actions that supplement and build on this six-step process. As an example, we provide one more case study of an organization that faced the need to change its culture. The key to culture change in this organization, however, was certain actions taken by the top management team that complemented the OCAI methodology. We discuss this case in order to illustrate variations that are possible when the OCAI serves as the foundation but not the comprehensive strategy for culture change.

Supplementing the OCAI Methodology

The company we describe in this case was divided into a number of business divisions, each of which offered customers a different product or service. Thick boundaries existed among the divisions, and division managers functioned as the heads of their own kingdoms. In a discussion of the company's future, the CEO and the president of the business concluded that any customer should be able to effortlessly access all the company's products and services across different businesses. But such an outcome was completely fictitious at the present time. Since they wanted to present a seamless front to their customers, these two senior managers felt it was essential to begin with the top management team. They needed a team that really was a team. They knew that if the top managers continued to behave in fragmented, self-serving ways, the organization simply wouldn't survive over the long term. A new culture, emphasizing cooperation, teamwork, and customer service, was required.

Although everyone within the organization claimed to agree with this vision, little changed. Particularly troublesome were the division heads, who had learned to operate successfully in an independent manner and were quite uncomfortable with the concept of working cooperatively with one another. The president, who encountered continual resistance and increasing frustration as he worked with these division heads, asked one of us to join him as a change agent. Our charge was to help him change the organization's culture, beginning with the building of an effective top management team.

After engaging in interviews, analyzing company documents, and holding lengthy conversations with the president, we agreed that a deep culture change was necessary. Subsequently, one of us attended a two-day meeting with the management group. It was clear that this group was comprised of bright, well-intentioned people who wanted to fulfill the organization's objectives. They had initiated a number of rational steps to try to implement a change process. For example, they had rearranged boxes on the organizational chart, reconfigured reporting relationships, and written new policies. They were not, however, acting like a team.

Toward the end of the meeting, we discussed the team-building process together, and we planned a two-and-a-half-day meeting to work on team building. We decided to begin by analyzing the culture of the team. We would then employ a series of exercises to analyze and change the actual behavior of the team. We also planned a series of follow-up meetings designed to check on progress and to realign assignments, if necessary.

The head of human resources, a man who was also an experienced change agent, assisted in the team-building meeting. On the first morning, the group appeared uneasy. We began with the nonthreatening task of employing the OCAI to analyze the current and desired cultures within the organization. The group consisted of fifteen people, representing both line and staff functions. In the beginning of the cultural analysis process, three subgroups of five people were created. Each individual completed a personal analysis and then shared his or her results with the subgroup. Each subgroup compiled its results and shared them with the entire group. A comprehensive profile of these results appears in Figure 5.7.

The group members found that depicting the organization on a cultural profile was an easy and insightful exercise. Their results provided us with the material we needed for a discussion of where they were and where they needed to go. After the discussion, we asked them to return to their subgroups and carefully consider the meaning of change in each quadrant, as described earlier in this chapter. Their subgroup discussion was structured around this question: What does it mean and what does it not mean to increase, decrease, or stay the same in a quadrant? Using the form presented in Figure 5.4, they produced the results shown in Figure 5.8.

The group members were pleased with their lists and were consequently feeling very comfortable and confident. We indicated that this diagnostic process was consistent with their usual pattern of cognitive work and that they were now going to slowly move

Figure 5.7 Organizational Culture Profile for the Company in the Case Study

The Clan Culture

An organization that focuses on internal maintenance with flexibility, concern for people, and sensitivity to customers.

The Adhocracy Culture

An organization that focuses on external positioning with a high degree of flexibility and individuality.

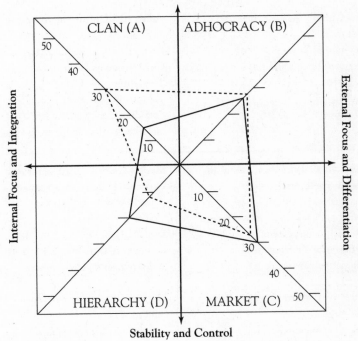

The Hierarchy Culture

An organization that focuses on internal maintenance with a need for stability and control.

The Market Culture

An organization that focuses on external positioning with a need for stability and control.

Preferred - - -
Now —

Figure 5.8 "Means–Does Not Mean" Analysis for the Company in the Case History

Clan Culture increase means:
More employee empowerment
More participation and involvement
More cross-functional teamwork
More horizontal communication
A more caring climate
More recognition for employees

Clan Culture increase does not mean:
A culture of "niceness"
Lack of standards and rigor
An absence of tough decisions
Slacking off
Tolerance of mediocrity

Adhocracy Culture increase means:
More employee suggestions
More process innovativeness
More thoughtful risk taking
Tolerance of first-time mistakes
More listening to customers

Adhocracy Culture increase does not mean:
Everyone for himself or herself
Covering up errors
Thoughtless risk taking
Taking our eye off the ball
Spending money on the latest fad
No coordination and sharing ideas

Hierarchy Culture decrease means:
Fewer sign-offs for decisions
More decentralized decisions
Fewer roadblocks and less red tape
Less micromanagement
Trying out more crazy ideas
Eliminating paperwork

Hierarchy Culture decrease does not mean:
Lack of measurement
Not holding people accountable
Not following the rules
Not monitoring performance
A nonorientation toward change

Market Culture decrease means:
Ongoing commitment to excellence
A world-class organization
Goal accomplishment
Energized employees
Less myopic thinking about targets
A less punishing environment

Market Culture decrease does not mean:
Less pressure for performance
Ceasing to listen to customers
Less satisfied customers
Missing deadlines
Lower quality standards
Less competitiveness

away from topics that were comfortable. We were going to slowly zero in on their own behavior.

They were asked to play a well-known simulation game called "Win as Much as You Can." Each person was required to contribute $20. Handing over their money seemed to increase their interest. The game is very simple and straightforward. It is based on the underlying (but nonobvious) premise that if all groups work together, they will all win money at the same rate. Eventually the bank goes broke, and the teams have all the money. But the game requires teamwork and in actual execution seldom involves much cooperation. Usually the groups each take a competitive stance and end up losing more than they win.

Our participants assumed that winning as much as you can meant that their own individual group should have more than any other group. The game rules allow this course of action, but it usually results in posturing and deceptive communication between groups. Once this plan is initiated, a single group may dominate the other groups, but the bank tends to accumulate the most money. Within moments of the start of the game, the entire group was engaged in exactly this kind of behavior. At the conclusion of the game, one group had deceived the other groups and won the most money.

As often happens in this exercise, the winning group waved its money in front of the losers and began to celebrate. As is also often the case, the other groups became deadly serious and began expressing moral outrage. The winning group was stunned and hurt. Its members quickly pointed out that the game was competitive and that winning was important. Their indignant opponents responded, "You either live by principle or you don't."

This game generated conflict and induced the entire group to consider some difficult issues about trust and cooperation. The discussion was exhausting. Afterward, we sent the participants outside to play volleyball. This was quite a departure from their normal work routine. These individuals would typically arrive at work at 7:00 A.M. and continue until 10:30 P.M. They paid little attention to their natural flow of energy, their level of activity, or their exhaustion.

The next morning, we asked the group members their opinion of the simulation game. Most of their comments centered on the premise that once trust is violated, it is extremely difficult to restore. We asked the group members what it meant to win as much as you can. There were a variety of answers. We indicated some dissatisfaction with their responses by repeating the question. Gradually, the group realized that had they honestly cooperated with one another, the entire group would have had all the money and the bank would have gone broke. This was true, of course, but they were still missing a vital point.

We asked them what they would have had besides the money. After a long pause, one person said, "Trust." We asked the participant to explain. He replied, "We would have had the money, but we would also have had a tremendous sense of pride and trust among ourselves. That would have given us the capacity to perform at a level we have never really experienced before. I think that trust might be a greater financial asset than money. Trust is the means and profit is the end. In pursuit of the golden egg, we often sacrifice the goose."

This was an important insight. People indicated that they had never considered an organization in that light. This led to an extensive and unusual discussion about cooperation and teamwork. They were beginning to see the value of trust.

As a follow-up step, participants were asked to list instances when they had taken part in a collective episode of high performance. They shared their lists with their subgroups and identified the characteristics of a high-performance team. The subgroup lists were consolidated and written on a flipchart.

We revealed that until now, all the activities, including the OCAI work, had just been a warm-up. Now the group was going to tackle the real challenges. Some people, we suggested, might not be up to it. We explained that their list of characteristics described a high-performance team and represented where they aspired to be. If they sincerely wanted to be a high-performance team, they would each have to make deep, personal change.

Each group member was given fourteen 5-by-7-inch cards. We explained a well-known intervention. On the front of each card, the group members were to write the name of one of the other fourteen people in the room. Below each name, they were to write the things they most appreciated and admired about the person—"Here is what I admire most about you." On the back of the card, they were to answer the following question: "If we are to seriously move from where we are today to become a high-performance team, what do I need from you that I am not currently getting?" (That is, how must this person change his or her behavior if we are to become a high-performance team?) This activity meant that each person in the group would receive fourteen cards with comments of appreciation and expectations for change.

The group was given ninety minutes to complete the exercise. The completed cards were distributed to each of the intended recipients. The recipients were then given forty-five minutes to read and analyze their own cards and to prepare a response regarding what they had learned and what change commitments they were ready to make.

The president was asked to go first in order to provide a role model for the entire group. If he ducked the pain of facing change, he would free the others to do the same. He stood up and reviewed the themes on his cards. He indicated what the group was asking of him and made some painful commitments that included performance measurements and follow-ups. It was a magnificent performance. One by one, everyone took a turn. It was a somber and reflective process. Several times people were close to tears.

At the conclusion of the session, the participants were emotionally exhausted, so they were sent to play volleyball again. Here a serendipitous event occurred. Their skill level and ability to participate as teams was several levels higher than it had been the day before. The next morning, we pointed out this observation and asked everyone why their play had improved. After some contemplation, they indicated that their trust level was much higher. They felt more cooperative and had more confidence in themselves and their team members. They felt that these factors increased their ability to perform.

We reflected on the need for personal change and then engaged in a storytelling exercise. All team members identified three experiences in which they had seen an organizational culture actually altered, and they described in detail how it unfolded. Each person took a turn telling one story, and we went three times around the group. This process was both insightful and stimulating. From their own experiences, team members began to more fully understand the need for personal behavior change. A discussion followed highlighting the lessons learned, the principles for action uncovered, and the insights for personal behavior change. Participants themselves suggested the need for setting a personal example for the organization, and they committed to the notion of holding themselves accountable by keeping a journal of their own behavior over the next year.

In the final session, we returned to the original task of planning cultural change. The group engaged the OCAI step of creating an action agenda. They identified and committed to specific structures, processes, and behaviors that needed to be altered. Their plan came together quickly and reflected a surprising consensus.

Two weeks later, one of the participants reflected, "In my whole career, I have never had a developmental experience that powerful. Several of us were recently on the corporate plane returning from Washington. You could tell that we weren't the same. The difference in our relationships is palpable."

The initial sessions with this organization were the beginning of their team-building process and the initiation of the cultural change process. These processes continued during our follow-up meetings. The participants often used their OCAI map of current and preferred culture as a point of reference. Yet they sensed a need to continue the process and not stop at the formulation of the OCAI profiles and strategies. They wanted to keep moving forward, and they talked of being ready to confront some of their deeper issues. The trouble was, they simply did not know how. This group, like nearly all groups, had a problem with what Chris Argyris (1993) calls "undiscussable issues." An undiscussable issue is one that is important to the group but is too threatening to discuss within the group. This group called its undiscussable issues "sacred cows." Group members believed that they were blocked by a number of sacred cows and really wanted to confront them.

During our first follow-up meeting, the participants were asked to reflect on their experience with undiscussable issues. They were to analyze what constitutes an undiscussable issue and what the resulting consequences are. The following four questions and answers are a consolidation of their conclusions.

1. *Why do undiscussable issues exist?* Sometimes an undiscussable issue exists because of historical events. When the issue first surfaced, tempers may have flared and personal attacks may have been made. The group probably sensed that it did not have the ability to productively confront the issue and so avoided it. Sometimes the issue never surfaces again at all. One or more group members may send an implicit message that says, "This is an issue that must not be raised. If it is, I will be deeply hurt or uncontrollably angry."

Sometimes an issue originates as a threat from outside the company. To evaluate it would be to consider something too painful to acknowledge. Denial is seen as absolutely necessary. The group implicitly agrees to never consider the issue. Anyone who dares to raise it, by definition, puts himself or herself outside the group. When these dynamics occur, people rationalize their actions so as to avoid confronting and resolving the issues. They argue that it is more painful to raise the issue than to live with it. There could be no successful resolution anyway.

2. *What are the costs of undiscussable issues?* When undiscussable issues arise, people segment or categorize their responses into legitimate and illegitimate categories. Basic honesty and openness are sacrificed. Communication becomes segmented in that cognitive and emotional messages cease to be congruent. Exchanges become intellectual but with little emotional complement. People show little

enthusiasm. They talk, but their words are empty. The value of the information that is exchanged drops. The process becomes inefficient. Time is spent and information is exchanged, but cohesive achievement does not occur. Value is not added. Trust falls, and transaction costs go up. Only the easiest, most consensual decisions are made. Innovation becomes unlikely. People withdraw. The group segments into coalitions, and backstage political action increases. Trust and respect begin to decay. People are categorized, and their behavior is often labeled with negative meaning. Perceptions become self-fulfilling prophecies. Cancerous, vicious cycles set in. Individuals often have difficulty describing what is taking place, but they feel disempowered and helpless. The group moves toward a threatening situation with the individual members having little choice but to deny all the ongoing behavior that is driving them toward a crisis.

Groups generate the most energy when they are stretching and successfully negotiating the external challenges they face. Success is a function of creative congruence between internal and external realities. It is less likely to occur when there are significant undiscussable issues in the group.

3. *Why do we not confront undiscussable issues?* A discussion would threaten the trust and cohesion of the group. Individuals fear that they will be unable to function effectively as a group if they probe deeply into an issue associated with such a high level of potential conflict. Individually, the potential discussion is seen as a threat to self-esteem, credibility, and job security. Anticipation of such a discussion stimulates feelings of fear, anxiety, stress, tension, embarrassment, and pain. Undiscussable issues are avoided because they produce personal as well as organizational pain.

4. *What actions should a group take to deal with undiscussable issues?* Relying on a foundation of trust in the team—a product of previous steps in the culture change process—obtain perceptions from team members of what the undiscussable issues might be. Make a written list, and clarify the wording of each issue so that everyone agrees that it is captured accurately.

Sometimes the most important part of discussing an undiscussable issue is understanding clearly what the issue is. A clear and precise definition of the issue is a key first step. Once the issues are defined and articulated, identify which team members need to be a part of each issue discussion. Not every issue may require the attention of the entire team. In order to build capability and trust, attack the easiest issues first.

Before honest and open discussion of undiscussable issues can occur, the importance of the group and its mission must be rearticulated and reinforced. This is because undiscussable issues threaten to produce change, loss, and pain, and people are willing to incur personal loss for the good of the group only if they believe in its purpose and mission. They are willing to suffer a loss if they can be a part of an even more vital and successful group. Once discussion has begun on an issue, it is important that the group stay with it until a strategy has been identified to address the issue or it has been resolved. The group must be dogged in confronting issues while at the same time must be deeply caring and concerned about individual members. Group members must recognize the need to balance honest, straightforward, challenging talk with supportive communication and an expression of personal concern. This balance is predicated on a belief in the sensitivity, fairness, and integrity of the group members and of the central authority figures. Because individuals may experience some kind of a loss or personal threat in this discussion, it is important to help people feel supported, fairly treated, listened to, and understood. Individual and group confidentiality and integrity need to be carefully maintained.

These observations provided us with a guide for moving ahead. Launching the team on its journey of change was another matter. With considerable reservation, we made a list of the undiscussable issues. We prioritized the ten issues on the list and began to address them one by one. The discussions took several meetings. Many tense and uncomfortable moments occurred, but the team kept moving forward.

Today this team is not perfect. Yet it continues to improve on multiple fronts. It is an entirely different group than the one with which we started. It is doubtful that anyone at the time of the first meeting could have imagined the team's present level of effectiveness and competence. In order to reach the current level of performance, the team members had to make some difficult decisions. Initially, they were personally committed to culture change and high team performance. Along the way, however, they paid a high price. They discovered that deep change at the collective level requires deep change at the personal level. Yet in order for personal change to occur, they had to feel safe at the outset of the process, and they had to experience some small successes before they could confront more risky issues. This is exactly what the OCAI allowed us to accomplish in the initial stages of this intervention.

6

INDIVIDUAL CHANGE AS A KEY TO CULTURE CHANGE

As illustrated in Chapter Five, without personal behavior change on the part of the organization's members, organizational culture change will be frustrated. A change in culture, in the end, depends on the implementation of behaviors by individuals in the organization that reinforce the new cultural values and are consistent with them. It is possible to identify a desired culture and to specify strategies and activities designed to produce change, but without the change process becoming personalized, without individuals' being willing to engage in new behaviors, without an alteration in the managerial competencies demonstrated in the organization, the organization's fundamental culture will not change. This chapter extends the Competing Values Framework to include a process by which managerial behaviors—that is, the skills and competencies of managers—can be changed to reinforce the culture change process.

This process of individual change reinforcing cultural change has been used in organizations throughout the world over the past decade. It is based on the Management Skills Assessment Instrument (MSAI) provided in Appendix B. The MSAI and the improvement process described in this chapter have served as the foundation for the University of Michigan's Management of Manager's program, which *Business Week* rated as one of the five best executive education programs in the United States. The instrument and methodology have also been used in many Fortune 500 companies and in firms in Europe, Asia, and South America. A variety of government, health care, and educational organizations have adopted this process to facilitate culture change as well as to foster improvement in managerial leadership. The MSAI instrument is copyrighted, and permission is required for its broad use, but it is reproduced in Appendix B to help individuals interested in a full-fledged change effort to be as comprehensive as possible in their approach.

For those interested in the validity and reliability of the MSAI, a brief explanation of the psychometric properties of the instrument is provided in Appendix B.

In the following sections, we first identify the individual management skills and competencies that are crucial for effective managerial performance, and we then show how they are congruent with the Competing Values Framework. Next, we introduce the MSAI and identify a methodology for creating a managerial skills profile. This profile, because it is based on the same framework as the organizational culture profile, can be used to identify which skills and competencies managers must develop or improve in order to enhance the culture change effort. A process is then described for developing personal improvement agendas in order to assist managers in accomplishing desired personal change.

Critical Management Skills

It has been a long time since unbridled growth, readily accessible resources, and a seemingly unlimited supply of easily satisfied customers were typical of the environments of most business organizations. Under those conditions—typical of the 1960s and 1970s—inexperienced, sloppy, and even ineffective management could be hidden. The organization's successes made up for the frailties of poorly prepared managers. Managerial mistakes—in addition to waste, redundancy, and inefficiency—were overshadowed by constant increases in revenues and sales. The modern environment of organizations, however, is no longer so benevolent. Razor-sharp managerial leadership is required now just to stay even. Under conditions of lean resources, escalating competition, and hyperturbulent change, management mistakes and inadequacies are often both visible and consequential. Never has there been a period of time when effective managerial leadership is more crucial for organizational success.

But what is effective managerial leadership? If culture change is to be enhanced, what kinds of behaviors need to be targeted? On what specific skills should improvement efforts be focused? How can managers' competencies be improved to facilitate organizational culture change?

Extensive research by several management scholars, including our own work, has identified managerial leadership skills that characterize the most effective managers and the most effective organizations worldwide. A summary of fifteen of those studies is found in Whetten and Cameron (2005), which presents lists of critical skills from a variety of surveys of managers and leaders. In one study, for example, Whetten and Cameron interviewed over four hundred individuals named by top executives as the most effective managers in their organizations. These highly effective executives were asked to identify the skills they considered the most crucial for their success. Questions such as the following were asked: Who fails and who succeeds in your organization, and why? If you selected someone to take your place, what skills would you make certain that that person possessed? What skills are demonstrated by the managers you most admire? What critical competencies must managers have in your company to move up? These interviews produced a list of approximately forty critical skills that they thought typified the most effective managers in the most effective organizations. A variety of other studies identified additional competencies (see Whetten and Cameron, 2005), but not surprisingly, a large overlap exists in the lists produced by these studies. It is relatively easy to identify a common set of managerial leadership competencies that characterize effective managers.

We clustered the skills and competencies that emerged from these multiple studies into a set of competency categories applicable mainly to mid-level and upper-level managers. These competencies are appropriate primarily for managers who manage managers. They may be somewhat less relevant for first-line supervisors. These categories are not considered comprehensive by any means, but they do summarize many of the critically important managerial leadership competencies typical of effective mid- and upper-level managers. That is, these skills have been identified in multiple studies as being key to managerial effectiveness. The competency categories are listed in Figure 6.1. These competency categories are organized by the Competing Values Framework so that three categories fit into each quadrant of the model. The twelve categories represent clusters of competencies—multiple skills are subsumed under each category title—and individual items on the MSAI assess the extent to which managers effectively demonstrate these competencies.

The twelve competency categories are as follows:

Clan Skills

- *Managing teams*—facilitating effective, cohesive, smooth-functioning, high-performance teamwork
- *Managing interpersonal relationships*—facilitating effective interpersonal relationships, including supportive feedback, listening, and resolution of interpersonal problems

Figure 6.1 Critical Managerial Competencies

Flexibility and Discretion

Culture Type: CLAN	Culture Type: ADHOCRACY
Managing teams	Managing innovation
Managing interpersonal relationships	Managing the future
Managing the development of others	Managing continuous improvement
Culture Type: HIERARCHY	Culture Type: MARKET
Managing acculturation	Managing competitiveness
Managing the control system	Energizing employees
Managing coordination	Managing customer service

Internal Focus and Integration ← → External Focus and Differentiation

Stability and Control

- *Managing the development of others*—helping individuals improve their performance, expand their competencies, and obtain personal development opportunities

Adhocracy Skills

- *Managing innovation*—encouraging individuals to innovate, expand alternatives, become more creative, and facilitate new idea generation
- *Managing the future*—communicating a clear vision of the future and facilitating its accomplishment
- *Managing continuous improvement*—fostering an orientation toward continuous improvement, flexibility, and productive change among individuals in their work life

Market Skills

- *Managing competitiveness*—fostering competitive capabilities and an aggressive orientation toward exceeding competitors' performance
- *Energizing employees*—motivating and inspiring individuals to be proactive, to put forth extra effort, and to work vigorously
- *Managing customer service*—fostering an orientation toward serving customers, involving them, and exceeding their expectations

Hierarchy Skills

- *Managing acculturation*—helping individuals become clear about what is expected of them, what the culture and standards of the organization are, and how they can best fit into the work setting
- *Managing the control system*—ensuring that procedures, measurements, and monitoring systems are in place to keep processes and performance under control
- *Managing coordination*—fostering coordination within the organization as well as with external units and managers and sharing information across boundaries

The instrument that assesses these skill competencies (the MSAI in Appendix B) is behaviorally based in that it assesses managerial behaviors and actions. It does not measure managerial style or attitudes. It is difficult, if not impossible, to change managerial styles; the important changes needed to support cultural change are the behaviors of managers and organization members. For culture change to occur, in other words, the actions of managers must change (they must "walk the talk"). The MSAI helps managers identify their own current managerial strengths and weaknesses as well as the competencies that will help the organization move toward the preferred future culture. A key showing which MSAI items are associated with which culture quadrant is provided at the end of Appendix B to help readers diagnose their own competency and cultural match. To accomplish a complete diagnosis, however, a more comprehensive process should be used.

Here's how it works.

Personal Management Skills Profile

Managers involved in the culture change initiative complete the MSAI themselves. Then each manager gives a version of the instrument—the Associates Rating Form—to a sample of his or her subordinates, peers, and superiors. (Usually we encourage individuals to use four subordinates, four peers, and at least one superior for a total of at least nine associates.) These individuals provide ratings of the extent to which the focal manager demonstrates behaviors associated with the critical competencies. In other words, each manager receives information on the extent to which he or she is effectively performing the critical managerial leadership competencies based on self-ratings and the ratings of subordinates, peers, and superiors. This is generally known as *360-degree feedback.*

A feedback report is prepared and provided to the managers in which comparisons are made between the manager's own self-ratings and the ratings of his or her associates. The feedback report also presents a comparison of the scores provided by the manager's associates with the scores of approximately eighty thousand other managers who have completed the instrument. This comparison is in the form of a percentile rank so that managers can see how they compare to managers worldwide on each managerial competency. An example of a summary feedback report is provided in Exhibit 6.1.

The data provided in Exhibit 6.1 summarize one manager's competency category scores. At the left are listed the twelve competency categories on the MSAI. The scores for each competency are averages of five questionnaire items that relate to individual

Exhibit 6.1 Managerial Information Summary (Feedback Report)

Scale	Self-Rating (mean)	Others' Scores (mean)	Others' Scores Rank (percentile)
Clan Quadrant	4.27	3.28	14
Managing teams	4.60	3.20	14
Managing interpersonal relationships	4.00	3.55	24
Managing the development of others	4.20	3.10	9
Adhocracy Quadrant	4.40	3.53	32
Managing innovation	4.20	3.65	29
Managing the future	4.60	3.53	49
Managing continuous improvement	4.40	3.43	22
Market Quadrant	4.13	3.66	49
Managing competitiveness	3.80	3.54	51
Energizing employees	4.00	3.88	65
Managing customer service	4.60	3.55	32
Hierarchy Quadrant	3.80	3.31	16
Managing acculturation	3.40	3.18	14
Managing the control system	4.00	3.48	26
Managing coordination	4.00	3.28	13

Note: Self-rating and others' scores are based on a scale of 1 (low) to 5 (high); see Exhibit 6.2.

skills within each category. For example, the score associated with the "managing teams" category is an average of the five items assessing competency in effectively managing teams on the MSAI. The average score associated with the quadrant is an average of the fifteen items that are contained in that particular quadrant.

The manager's self-ratings and others' scores are on a scale of 1 (low) to 5 (high). Thus the higher the score, the more competent or effective the person is rated. For example, the manager featured in Exhibit 6.1 rated himself an average of 4.27 in the clan quadrant skills, 4.40 in the adhocracy quadrant skills, 4.13 in the market quadrant skills, and 3.80 in the hierarchy quadrant skills. His self-rating scores indicate that he considers himself to be strongest in the managerial competencies related to the adhocracy quadrant. His second-highest self-ratings are in the clan quadrant. His highest self-rating scores are associated with the three areas of competency in the adhocracy quadrant (ratings of 4.2 for managing innovation, 4.6 for managing the future, and 4.4 for managing continuous improvement) and the three areas of competency in the clan quadrant (ratings of 4.6 for managing teams, 4.0 for managing interpersonal relationships, and 4.2 for managing the development of others).

From the ratings of the manager's subordinates, peers, and superiors—combined, averaged, and presented under "Others' Scores"—we can see that this manager's associates rate him as strongest in the market quadrant and least effective in the clan quadrant. A clear discrepancy exists between the way the manager perceives himself and the way he is perceived by his associates. Relatively speaking, his associates rate this manager as weakest in the quadrant in which he rates himself as performing quite effectively. This may suggest an area for targeted self-improvement.

It is also notable that the manager's self-ratings are higher than the associates' ratings in each competency category. This is the usual result pattern in the MSAI scores. Most managers rate themselves higher than they are rated by their associates. More will be said about the significance of these mismatches later. For now, it suffices to point out that these ratings help the manager get an overall picture of his managerial strengths and weaknesses. That is, he can see the extent to which the people with whom he works hold the same opinion of his managerial strengths and weaknesses as he does.

The final column in Exhibit 6.1 compares the scores this manager received from his associates to the scores of other managers worldwide. For example, the score of 3.20 on "managing teams" is at the 14th percentile. This means 14 percent of managers receive lower scores than 3.20, and 86 percent receive higher scores. Although he considers it to be one of his strongest areas (giving himself a 4.6 rating), the scores from his associates put him at a quite low level compared to managers worldwide. This may also suggest an area for targeted self-improvement.

Many managers are tempted to interpret the percentile column like a final grade in school or like an overall performance appraisal rating. They think of it as an evaluation of their effectiveness or goodness as a manager. That is an inappropriate way to view these percentile data. The absolute magnitude of the percentile scores may be biased by associates who have a tendency to avoid 1 or 5 in responding to any question or by a tendency to use only 1 or 5 in responding to items. It may also be biased by a tendency in the organization itself to rate everyone high (as when everyone receives a 4 or a 5 in annual performance appraisals) or by a tendency to rate everyone low in the organization (as when hardly anyone gets 4s and 5s) or by a single associate who gives all extremely low or all extremely high scores. In other words, some response bias may be present in the ratings affecting the absolute percentile score. A percentile rank of 88 may or may not indicate that the manager really is more effective than 88 percent of all other managers worldwide. The absolute value of the percentile rank could be biased in some way by the particular respondents selected. The best way to interpret these data, therefore, is to look for aberrations from the general trends—that is, especially high or especially low percentiles— so that areas needing improvement can be identified. The most appropriate way for the manager to use the data in this feedback report is to identify competencies needing improvement and competencies in which change can facilitate the desired culture shift.

Figure 6.2 displays a management skills profile for this manager's data. The scores on the feedback report are plotted on a Competing Values Framework grid. The resulting profile makes it easy to see the areas of greatest discrepancy between the manager's self-ratings and associates' ratings, the areas of strongest competency and weakest competency (the highest and lowest scores), and the extent to which the manager's skills are aligned with his organization's culture profile. Managers can use this profile to help identify areas for personal managerial improvement as well as to target competencies required for the culture change effort.

In addition to the data that show an average score for each competency area, more detailed feedback reports are also provided to managers. These pages provide feedback on each individual item on the MSAI. The reports divide the associates into separate subgroups—subordinates, peers, and superiors. Exhibit 6.2 shows the clan quadrant feedback report for this particular manager, and Figure 6.3 shows the management skills profile for the items that fall into this quadrant. The clan quadrant profile in Figure 6.3 compares the manager's self-ratings to the ratings of all associates in combination on each numbered statement in the clan quadrant.

In the feedback report in Exhibit 6.2, the individual items in the MSAI are listed on the left. The left-hand column of numbers shows the manager's own self-ratings on each item. The three columns headed "All Others" show (1) the mean scores on each item for all associates in combination, (2) the highest score and the lowest score received on each item (labeled "Range"), and (3) the percentile rank comparing the score on each item to those of other managers. Since the standard deviation for each item is approximately 0.5, managers can determine the extent to which significant differences exist between their own scores and those of their associates. *Differences larger than 1.0 are usually statistically significant.* The next columns divide the manager's associates into subgroups. Two columns headed "Subordinates" show just the subordinates' mean score and range, the "Peers" columns show the mean and range for the manager's peers, and the "Superiors" columns show the mean and range for the manager's boss (in this particular profile, only one superior participated). It is clear that whereas this manager's boss believes he is performing quite effectively in clan quadrant skills (most scores are 4 or 5), the subordinates' scores are significantly lower (the means range from 2.6 to 4.0). Peers' scores are between the superior's and the subordinates'.

The value of this feedback for a manager is that it identifies specific behaviors that should be addressed if change in managerial competency is to occur. The individual MSAI items each identify effective managerial behaviors based on research from the multiple research studies mentioned earlier. By identifying the competencies in need of improvement, this manager's own effectiveness can be increased.

The clan quadrant profile depicted in Figure 6.3 helps clarify the discrepancies and point up this manager's relative strengths and weaknesses. Pictorial representations of the data almost always improve understanding and clarity. It is apparent from this profile that the manager is in need of the most improvement on items 5, 18, 21, 22, 23, 25, and 47. That is, associates' scores are lowest and discrepancies are highest on these specific managerial behaviors. Improving skill in these competencies can help the manager improve his overall effectiveness. However, in addition to this general improvement motive, competencies must also be identified that help reinforce the culture change effort. That additional step is described next.

Personal Improvement Agendas

As indicated earlier, 360-degree feedback has two important purposes. One is to assist the manager in improving managerial leadership competency. The other is to identify the competencies most needed to support the organizational culture change process. To assist managers in identifying the managerial competencies that will be most beneficial to the development of a future culture, the preferred organizational culture profile (see Figure 2.2) is compared to the current personal management skills profile. For example, the manager serving as our example in this chapter is part of a top-level

Figure 6.2 Management Skills Profile

Clan Culture Leadership Roles

The Facilitator is people- and process-oriented. This person manages conflict and seeks consensus. His or her influence is based on getting people involved in the decision making and problem solving. Participation and openness are actively pursued.

The Mentor is caring and empathic. This person is aware of others and cares for the needs of individuals. His or her influence is based on mutual respect and trust. Morale and commitment are actively pursued.

Adhocracy Culture Leadership Roles

The Innovator is clever and creative. This person envisions change. His or her influence is based on anticipation of a better future and generates hope in others. Innovation and adaptation are actively pursued.

The Visionary is future-oriented in thinking. This person focuses on where the organization is going and emphasizes possibilities as well as probabilities. Strategic direction and continuous improvement of current activities are hallmarks of this style.

Hierarchy Culture Leadership Roles

The Monitor is technically expert and well-informed. This person keeps track of all details and contributes expertise. His or her influence is based on information control. Documentation and information management are actively pursued.

The Coordinator is dependable and reliable. This person maintains the structure and flow of the work. His or her influence is based on situational engineering, managing schedules, giving assignments, physical layout, etc. Stability and control are actively pursued.

Market Culture Leadership Roles

The Competitor is aggressive and decisive. This person actively pursues goals and targets and is energized by competitive situations. Winning is a dominant objective, and the focus is on external competitors and marketplace position.

The Producer is task-oriented and work-focused. This person gets things done through hard work. His or her influence is based on intensity and rational arguments around accomplishing things. Productivity is actively pursued.

Figure 6.2   Management Skills Profile, Cont'd.

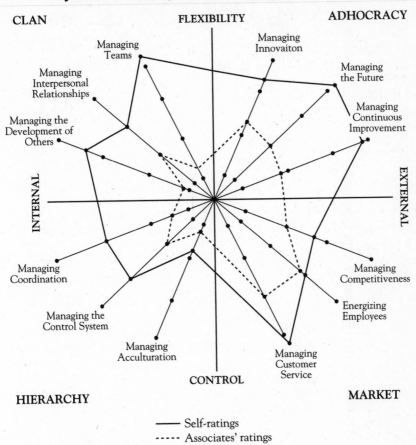

management team in a well-known European business. This team's "Now" and "Preferred" culture plots are shown in Figure 6.4. The team reached consensus on the culture profiles presented in the figure. As can be seen, the organization's current organizational culture is dominated by the adhocracy and market quadrants, whereas the preferred culture requires a shift toward the hierarchy and clan quadrants. This management team reasoned that more control and attention to efficient processes will be necessary for them to

Exhibit 6.2 Individual Question Feedback for the Clan Quadrant

Question	Self Mean	All Others Mean	All Others Range	All Others Percentile	Subordinates Mean	Subordinates Range	Peers Mean	Peers Range	Superiors Mean	Superiors Range
CLAN QUADRANT	**4.3**	3.3	2.4–4.0	14	3.0	2.4–3.5	3.6	3.5–3.7	4.0	4.0–4.0
Managing Teams	**4.6**	3.2	2.0–4.0	14	2.9	2.0–3.4	3.5	3.4–3.6	4.0	4.0–4.0
12. I build cohesive, committed teams of people.	5.0	3.3	2.0–4.0	26	3.0	2.0–4.0	3.5	3.0–4.0	4.0	4.0–4.0
18. I facilitate effective information sharing and problem solving in my group.	4.0	3.0	2.0–4.0	9	2.6	2.0–3.0	3.5	3.0–4.0	4.0	4.0–4.0
21. I create an environment where involvement and participation in decisions are encouraged and rewarded.	5.0	3.3	2.0–4.0	17	3.0	2.0–4.0	3.5	3.0–4.0	4.0	4.0–4.0
22. In groups I lead, I make sure that sufficient attention is given to both task accomplishment and interpersonal relationships.	4.0	3.1	2.0–4.0	15	2.8	2.0–3.0	3.5	3.0–4.0	4.0	4.0–4.0
49. When leading a group, I ensure collaboration and positive conflict resolution among group members.	5.0	3.4	2.0–4.0	20	3.2	2.0–4.0	3.5	3.0–4.0	4.0	4.0–4.0

Question	Self Mean	All Others			Subordinates		Peers		Superiors	
		Mean	Range	Percentile	Mean	Range	Mean	Range	Mean	Range
Managing Interpersonal Relationships	4.0	3.6	2.4–4.2	24	3.3	2.4–4.0	3.9	3.8–4.0	4.2	4.2–4.2
1. I communicate in a supportive way when people in my unit share their problems with me.	4.0	3.8	2.0–4.0	20	3.6	2.0–4.0	4.0	4.0–4.0	4.0	4.0–4.0
13. I give my subordinates regular feedback about how I think they're doing.	4.0	3.4	2.0–5.0	31	2.8	2.0–4.0	4.0	4.0–4.0	5.0	5.0–5.0
23. When giving negative feedback to others. I foster their self-improvement rather than defensiveness or anger.	4.0	3.1	2.0–4.0	16	2.6	2.0–4.0	4.0	4.0–4.0	4.0	4.0–4.0
48. I listen openly and attentively to others who give me their ideas, even when I disagree.	4.0	3.9	3.0–5.0	42	4.0	3.0–5.0	3.5	3.0–4.0	4.0	4.0–4.0
50. I foster trust and openness by showing understanding for the point of view of individuals who come tome with problems or concerns.	4.0	3.6	2.0–5.0	28	3.4	2.0–5.0	4.0	4.0–4.0	4.0	4.0–4.0

Exhibit 6.2 Individual Question Feedback for the Clan Quadrant, Cont'd.

Question	Self Mean	All Others Mean	All Others Range	All Others Percentile	Subordinates Mean	Subordinates Range	Peers Mean	Peers Range	Superiors Mean	Superiors Range
Managing the Development of Others										
5. I regularly coach subordinates to improve their management skills so they can achieve higher levels of performance.	4.2	3.1	2.0–3.8	9	2.9	2.0–3.8	3.3	3.2–3.4	3.8	3.8–3.8
20. I make sure that others in my unit are provided with opportunities for personal growth and development.	4.0	2.8	2.0–4.0	8	2.6	2.0–4.0	3.0	3.0–3.0	3.0	3.0–3.0
24. I give others assignments and responsibilities that provide opportunities for their personal growth and development.	4.0	3.5	2.0–4.0	25	3.2	2.4–4.0	4.0	4.0–4.0	4.0	4.0–4.0
25. I actively help prepare others to move up in the organization.	5.0	3.3	2.0–4.0	7	2.8	2.0–4.0	4.0	4.0–4.0	4.0	4.0–4.0
47. I facilitate a work environment where peers as well as subordinates learn from and help develop one another.	4.0	3.0	2.0–4.0	12	3.0	2.0–4.0	2.5	2.0–3.0	4.0	4.0–4.0

Note: Scores are based on the following scale: 5 = strongly agree, 4 = moderately agree, 3 = slightly agree or slightly disagree, 2 = moderately disagree, and 1 = strongly disagree.

Figure 6.3 Management Skills Profile for the Clan Quadrant

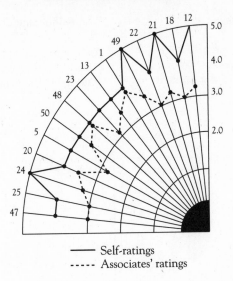

—— Self-ratings
----- Associates' ratings

successfully compete in their global marketplace. Getting the organization's systems under control, emphasizing efficiency, and pursuing cost containment along with enhancing the involvement, empowerment, and cohesion of the workforce led this team to conclude that an organizational culture change is needed.

The challenge of the manager in this example, therefore, is to develop a personal improvement agenda that will result in increased skill competency in the areas required by the future culture. To help him do that, a comparison is made between his management skills profile in Figure 6.2 and his team's preferred culture profile in Figure 6.4. It is important for this manager not to abandon his current managerial competencies, of course, but he may need to increase his skill in some competency areas that he has deemphasized or ignored until now. The discrepancy between his strongest areas of personal competency and the requirements of the future culture are obvious. The manager's associates give him the lowest scores in the hierarchy and clan quadrant competencies, but those are precisely the quadrants that are to be emphasized in the future by the

Figure 6.4 Organizational Culture Profile for the European Company

The Clan Culture

An organization that focuses on internal maintenance with flexibility, concern for people, and sensitivity to customers.

The Adhocracy Culture

An organization that focuses on external positioning with a high degree of flexibility and individuality.

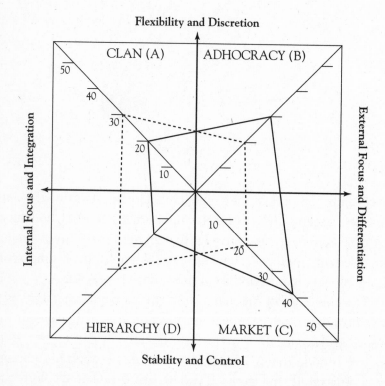

organization. Either the shift of culture will make this manager's competency profile less relevant and he will become less valuable to the firm in the future, or he will need to increase his effectiveness in the competency areas that support the hierarchy and clan quadrants. This means that the manager must develop skill in some new areas of competency.

The trouble is, how can he improve in an area that has not been emphasized in the past or about which he knows little? How can his skills be enhanced in competencies that are currently underdeveloped? This is the main purpose of using the 360-degree feed-back from the MSAI. The process of improving personal managerial competencies can be approached systematically by (1) identifying the specific skills requiring improvement or development, (2) designing an improvement plan that will lead to measurable progress, and (3) ensuring that the new set of managerial competencies reinforces and supports the culture change process.

To identify the specific skills to be improved and to assist in formulating a personal development plan, a series of questions in worksheet form is provided to the manager. These questions help highlight competency areas that the manager may not be aware of without looking carefully at the discrepancies between his own and his associates' ratings, the ranges in associates' perceptions, and his highest and lowest scores. They help the manager reduce the number of items that he must consider in his improvement plan to the few that are the most surprising and the most relevant. Twelve questions help guide this process:

1. On which items are the discrepancies the greatest between your own ratings and those of your associates?

2. On which items are there large discrepancies among the subgroups of your associates (your subordinates, peers, and superiors)?

3. On which items are there a wide range of responses, suggesting a lack of consistency in perceptions among your associates?

4. Based on your scores on the various items, in which competencies are you especially strong?

5. In what competencies does the most improvement seem to be indicated?

6. On the basis of your "Now" and "Preferred" organizational culture profile, what competencies in this quadrant should you most emphasize?

7. After reviewing the feedback from this quadrant as a whole, what specific managerial competencies would you most like to improve?

8. What specific suggestions from the list in Appendix D will help you improve the competencies you have identified?

9. What other specific actions can you take to help you improve these competencies?

10. When will these actions be started, and when will they be completed?

11. Who else must get involved to help you accomplish your action agenda, and what other resources do you need?

12. How will you know you've succeeded? What will be the indicators of success?

To assist managers in identifying specific actions to improve a specific competency area, lists of suggestions are provided. These are reproduced in Appendix D. These suggestions have been generated from managers over the past several years who offered advice regarding actions that helped them improve their own competency in a quadrant. They are not intended as a comprehensive list of suggestions or even a prescriptive list for many managers. At least some suggestions have proved useful, however, to most managers who have engaged in personal improvement and in organizational culture change efforts. They may be more useful as thought starters than as prescriptions.

To ensure that the managerial competencies identified in the personal improvement plan are aligned with the demands of the future organizational culture, we encourage managers to share their plan with their management team members. Three discussion questions may be addressed in such a meeting:

1. If I make substantial improvement in these competency areas—if I accomplish my personal improvement plan— will it facilitate our moving the organizational culture in the desired direction?

2. Will members of this management team support my own personal change efforts and hold me accountable for improvement?

3. What suggestions for change and improvement do you have
   that supplement my own action agenda?

The intent of these questions is for the manager to encourage the
management team to serve as a support group in moving toward the
desired behavioral and cultural changes. To repeat, without personal behavioral change on the part of managers, culture change is
impossible. A social support network to foster such behavioral
change is facilitated by the sharing of personal improvement plans
relating to critical managerial competencies.

7

A CONDENSED FORMULA FOR ORGANIZATIONAL CULTURE CHANGE

We have pointed out that almost all organizations develop a dominant type of organizational culture. They tend to emphasize one or more of four culture types—adhocracy, clan, hierarchy, or market culture. Particular types of cultures form as a result of certain values, assumptions, and priorities becoming dominant as the organization addresses challenges and adjusts to changes. These dominant cultures help the organization become more consistent and stable as well as more adaptable and flexible in dealing with its rapidly changing environment. Whereas these culture types tend to evolve in predictable ways over time, organizations face the need to change cultures in connection with many other forms of organizational change. Without a change in culture, most change initiatives, such as TQM, downsizing, reengineering, and teamwork, fall short of expectations. The first six chapters have laid out a process and methodology for effectively managing a change in organizational culture, and instruments have been provided to help assess the current organizational culture, the future preferred organizational culture, and the managerial competencies needed to facilitate the change initiative. This final chapter summarizes an abbreviated listing of the key steps in that process. This list of steps is intended to serve as a checklist or a set of reminders, not as a comprehensive description of the process. To implement a culture change process in earnest, it is important to read Chapters One through Six.

Diagnosis

1. Complete the Organizational Culture Assessment Instrument (OCAI). Rate the way your organization is *right now*. Select as the focus of your ratings the organization that is the target of the culture change effort.

2. Other members of your team should also complete the OCAI by themselves.

3. Each team member should compute an organizational culture profile for the currently existing culture using procedures outlined in Chapter Two.

4. Hold a discussion as a team regarding the culture that characterizes your organization right now. Reach consensus regarding each person's organizational culture profile. Do not just average numbers.

5. Complete the OCAI again, this time rating the way your organization should be in the future.

6. Other members of your team should also complete the OCAI again, rating the preferred or future culture.

7. Each team member should compute an organizational culture profile for the preferred culture using procedures outlined in Chapter Two.

8. Hold a discussion as a team regarding the culture that should characterize your organization in the future. Reach consensus. Do not just average numbers. Make certain that all individuals' perspectives are heard regarding where and how the organization needs to change.

9. Compare the profiles of the "Now" and "Preferred" cultures. Identify the gaps that help identify the changes in culture that need to be initiated.

Interpretation

10. Plot each question on the OCAI on the forms in Chapter Four. Draw conclusions about your organization's culture type, the congruency of your culture, the strength of your culture,

and the comparisons between your culture and some norm groups. These comparisons will also help you identify the culture changes that may be required.

11. Identify what culture changes need to occur. Identify which quadrants will increase in emphasis and which will decrease in emphasis.

12. Identify what it *means* and what it *does not mean* to initiate the changes in culture being suggested. Complete the forms in Chapter Five.

13. Identify two or three incidents or events that illustrate the key values that you want to permeate the future organizational culture. Recount these incidents or events in story form so that they illustrate the core values needed in the preferred culture. These stories should capture the essence of the future culture.

14. Reach consensus on which actions should be started, which should be stopped, and which should be continued in order for the culture change process to begin.

Implementation

15. Rely on the ten principles of organizational change described in Chapter Five when designing specific change initiatives.

16. Identify a few key steps that can be implemented right away. Select the strategies that will begin the process of culture change and create visible results. Specify timetables, benchmarks, and accountability targets.

17. Design a communication strategy that opens two-way communication channels and keeps everyone informed of changes. This strategy will involve identifying how, when, where, and who will communicate the new cultural values. Plan on continuous and comprehensive communication.

18. Identify the various aspects of the organization that must be changed in order to reinforce the preferred culture change. Consider especially the "seven S's": structure, symbols, systems, staff, strategy, style of leaders, and skills of managers.

19. Personalize the culture change. Identify the behaviors and competencies that each team member will need to develop or improve to reflect the new culture.

20. To assist team members in identifying personal changes that will support the culture change, complete the Management Skills Assessment Instrument (MSAI) in Appendix B. A general idea of the match between your own managerial competencies and your organizational culture profile can be obtained by using the key provided there. However, scoring the MSAI and comparing scores with those of forty thousand other managers will require coordinating with the authors. Use the suggestions in Appendix D to create personal improvement plans to improve managerial competencies.

Changing an organization's culture is a very difficult endeavor, of course. It requires a great deal of commitment and dedication on the part of the management team to make it work. This sort of commitment and dedication is needed mainly when a mismatch exists between the organization's own performance and the requirements of customers, the environment, or standards of excellence. It also is required when the organization's leaders hold a vision of the future that requires a shift in the organization's direction. Under such circumstances, commitment to a culture change process is crucial to the future success of the organization.

The processes and instruments presented in this book will be very valuable tools in assisting managers initiate and facilitate that culture change process. They have certainly proved to be so in a large number of organizations worldwide. On the other hand, the real work in culture change, and the most difficult part by far, lies in the actual implementation and follow-up. Consequently, managers should interpret these tools and this process as a foundation for culture change but not assume that the job is completed by reaching step 20 on our list. Plan on a multiyear effort, and plan on returning to these steps more than once in the process.

Appendix A
Organizational Culture Assessment Instrument (OCAI): Definition, Dimensions, Reliability, and Validity

This appendix is provided for individuals interested in the validity, reliability, and effects of the Organizational Culture Assessment Instrument (OCAI). The information provided here is of a scholarly nature, and it is intended to provide background evidence for the credibility of the OCAI. It may not be necessary to read through this information if you are interested primarily in managing a cultural change process. The information presented here has been generated from several scientific studies of organizational culture using the OCAI.

Of course, for the OCAI to be useful, a high level of confidence must exist that it is a tool that can lead to effective culture change. That is, we must be reasonably certain that it really does measure important aspects of organizational culture (a question of validity), that it does so reliably, and that the aspects of culture being measured have some relationship to organizational performance. Moreover, we must be clear about what dimensions of organizational culture are being considered, why they are important, and what the results of an assessment tell us. In this appendix, we provide some scholarly background on the meaning of organizational culture and its key dimensions, and we review the results of several studies that demonstrate the statistical reliability and validity of the OCAI. We also summarize several studies that used the OCAI to examine the relationships between organizational culture and desirable outcomes such as organizational effectiveness, leadership success, organizational strategies, processes, and decision styles.

Importance of Organizational Culture Assessment

The need to diagnose and manage organizational culture is growing in importance partly because of an increasing need to merge and mold different organizations' cultures as structural changes have occurred (for instance, when units are consolidated, when downsizing and outsourcing eliminate parts of the organization, or when entire organizations merge). The escalating importance of culture is also partly a result of the increasing turbulence, complexity, and unpredictability of the external environments in which organizations operate. Organizations tend to develop a dominant organizational culture over time as they adapt and respond to challenges and changes in the environment (Schein, 1983; Sathe, 1983). Just as individuals who face threat, uncertainty, and ambiguity reassert their own habituated behavior with redoubled force (Staw, Sandelands, and Dutton, 1981; Weick, 1984), institutions also tend to respond to challenges by reasserting their core cultural values with added zeal. As competition, change, and pressure intensify for organizations, therefore, organizational culture is given more prominence and emphasis. This is because, paradoxically, organizational culture creates both stability and adaptability for organizations. It creates stability by being the glue that holds the organization together. Culture reinforces continuity and consistency in the organization through adherence to a clear set of consensual values. Culture also fosters adaptability by providing a clear set of principles to follow when designing strategies to cope with new circumstances. Clarifying core competence and strategic intent (Prahalad and Hamel, 1990) are prerequisites to organizational adaptability, and both are grounded squarely in the organization's unique culture.

Organizational culture assessment is increasingly important, therefore, because of the need to both change and maintain stability in the face of increasingly turbulent external environments. Having a diagnostic instrument to identify core organizational culture values can be an especially useful tool in the effective management of organizational change.

Issues in Assessing Organizational Culture

Numerous discussions in the scholarly literature review the conceptual boundaries and the theoretical foundations of organizational culture (see, for example, Deal and Kennedy, 1982; Geertz, 1983; Schein, 1983, 1985; Frost and others, 1991; Cameron and Ettington, 1988; Ott, 1989; Denison, 1990; Martin, 1992; and Trice and Beyer, 1993). Writers have pointed out several important controversies that characterize the concept of organizational culture. These controversies relate to how to precisely define culture (definitional issues), how to measure culture (measurement issues), and what key dimensions should characterize culture (dimensional issues). Instead of rehearsing these controversies in detail here, interested readers are encouraged to review one of the works cited in this paragraph for a more in-depth treatment. For our purposes, it is necessary merely to summarize those three issues so that it is clear what positions are represented by our approach to assessing organizational culture.

Definitional Issues

The two main disciplinary foundations of organizational culture are summarized in Table A.1. Note that the concept of organizational culture emerged initially from two different disciplinary roots: an anthropological foundation (the fact that organizations *are* cultures) and a sociological foundation (the fact that organizations *have* cultures). Within each of these disciplines, two different approaches to

Table A.1 The Two Main Disciplinary Foundations of Organizational Culture

	Anthropological Foundation	*Sociological Foundation*
Functional Approach		
Focus	Collective behavior	Collective behavior
Investigator	Diagnostician, stays neutral	Diagnostician, stays neutral
Observation	Objective factors	Objective factors
Variable	Dependent (understand culture by itself)	Independent (culture predicts other outcomes)
Assumption	Organizations *are* cultures	Organizations *have* cultures
Semiotic Approach		
Focus	Individual cognitions	Individual cognitions
Investigator	Natives, do not stay neutral	Natives, do not stay neutral
Observation	Participant immersion	Participant immersion
Variable	Dependent (understand culture by itself)	Independent (culture predicts other outcomes)
Assumption	Organizations *are* cultures	Organizations *have* cultures

Note: The Competing Values Framework adopts the definition of culture represented by the functional, sociological tradition. Culture is treated as an attribute of the organization that can be measured separately from other organizational phenomena and, as we will show, can be very useful for predicting which organizations succeed and which do not. Culture is assumed to be an attribute of the organization itself and not merely a metaphor (such as bureaucracy, organized anarchy, or network) for labeling what an organization is. Adopting this assumption makes it necessary, however, to identify what aspects of culture are being considered and how the concept is being defined.

culture were developed: a functional approach (culture emerges from collective behavior) and a semiotic approach (culture resides in individual interpretations and cognitions). The primary distinctions summarized in Table A.1 are differences between culture defined as an attribute possessed by organizations and culture defined as a metaphor for describing organizations. The former approach assumes that researchers and managers can identify differences among organizational cultures, can change cultures, and can empirically measure cultures. The latter perspective assumes that nothing exists in organizations except culture, and one encounters culture anytime one rubs up against any organization. Culture is a potential predictor of other organizational outcomes (such as effectiveness) in the former perspective, whereas in the latter perspective it is a concept to be explained independent of any other phenomena.

Cameron and Ettington (1988) reviewed a long list of published definitions of organizational culture and noted that in a majority of cases, culture has been treated as an enduring set of values, beliefs, and assumptions that characterize organizations and their members (taking the functional, sociological perspective delineated in Table A.1). Most important, these definitions distinguish the concept of organizational *culture* from organizational *climate*, which refers to more temporary attitudes, feelings, and perceptions on the part of individuals. Culture is an enduring, slow-changing core attribute of organizations; climate, because it is based on attitudes, can change quickly and dramatically. Culture refers to implicit, often indiscernible aspects of organizations; climate refers to more overt, observable attributes of organizations. Culture includes core values and consensual interpretations about how things are; climate includes individualistic perspectives that are modified frequently as situations change and new information is encountered. The Competing Values approach described here focuses squarely on cultural attributes rather than climate attributes. We assess "how things are" in the organization rather than how individuals feel about them.

Measurement Issues

Using the term *organizational culture* helps differentiate the culture of the overall organization from the values, preferences, and inclinations of individuals (personal culture) and from the language, norms, and philosophies of a nation or civilization (societal culture). Organizations, of course, may have multiple, unique subcultures associated with different subunits. For example, the subculture of the marketing department may differ perceptibly from that of the engineering department, or a unionized employee subculture may appear to be different from the top management subculture. However, most organizational cultures are like holograms. In each separate element in a holographic image, unique information exists that differentiates that particular element from all others. Yet each element also contains common information from which the entire image can be reproduced. Similarly, organizational cultures may be comprised of unique subcultures, but each of these subcultures contains common attributes that make up an overarching culture typical of the entire organization. Assessing organizational culture means that the overarching elements are the focus of measurement, and the organization level of analysis is the intended target of assessment when using this instrument.

To measure culture at the organization level of analysis, three strategies are available: (1) a *holistic approach* in which the investigator becomes immersed in the culture and engages in in-depth participant observation; that is, the investigator tries to become a "native" in the organization; (2) *metaphorical or language approaches* in which the investigator uses language patterns in documents, reports, stories, and conversations to uncover cultural patterns, just as detectives use fingerprints, voice prints, or word prints to detect personal identity; and (3) *quantitative approaches* in which the investigator uses questionnaires or interviews to assess particular dimensions of culture. A quantitative approach allows multiple viewpoints to be considered in evaluating the attributes of an organization's culture.

Heated debates continue to rage among culture researchers about the best ways to assess culture. A central issue is whether a quantitative approach to culture assessment is valid or whether an in-depth, qualitative approach is the only way to detect and describe culture. The basic issue is this: when assessing culture via questionnaires or interviews, is one really measuring superficial characteristics of an organization—namely, organizational climate—rather than in-depth cultural values? Because culture is based on underlying values and assumptions, often unrecognized and unchallenged in organizations, one perspective argues that only by utilizing in-depth qualitative procedures in which artifacts, stories and myths, and interpretation systems are studied over long periods of time in a comprehensive way can cultural attributes be identified. "One must experience something to understand it" is the philosophical basis of this approach.

The opposing point of view argues that breadth of comparison is sacrificed by employing a qualitative approach. The investigation of multiple organizational cultures becomes impossible when immersion in each one is mandatory. To conduct comparisons among multiple cultures, quantitative approaches must be used. It is crucial, however, that the individuals responding to a survey instrument actually report underlying values and assumptions (culture) and not just superficial attitudes or perceptions (climate). This can be accomplished best, we argue, by using a *scenario analysis* procedure in which respondents report the extent to which written scenarios are indicative of their own organization's culture. These scenarios serve as cues—both emotionally and cognitively—that bring core cultural attributes to the surface. The old proverb "Fish discover water last" illustrates the philosophical basis of this approach. Respondents may be unaware of crucial attributes of culture until they are cued by the scenarios on the questionnaire. Numerous well-known studies of organizational culture have used this approach, including Ouchi and Johnson (1978), O'Reilly (1983), Denison (1990), and Cameron and Freeman (1991), and it is the one represented by the Competing Values approach to culture assessment.

Dimensional Issues

Since we can't pay attention to everything in an organization, it is necessary, in order to adequately diagnose organizational culture, to focus on certain dimensions of an organization's culture more than others. Two kinds of dimensions deserve brief mention here: *content* dimensions and *pattern* dimensions. Content dimensions refer to the aspects of an organization's culture that should be used as cues in scenarios in order to help individuals recognize their organization's cultural values. Pattern dimensions refer to a cultural profile that is produced by scoring a culture assessment instrument. Various dimensions on this profile can be used to diagnose culture.

Before explaining the content dimensions that comprise this instrument, an explanation of why these content dimensions can uncover organizational culture will be useful. That explanation relies on the notion of psychological archetypes.

Psychological theorists have pointed out that most individuals have a similar kind of framework for making sense of the world around them. This framework is called a *psychological archetype*, and it refers to the categories people form in their minds to organize the information they encounter. For example, Ian Mitroff (1983, p. 17) wrote:

> The more one examines the great diversity of world cultures, the more one finds that at the symbolic level there is an astounding amount of agreement between various archetypal images. People may disagree and fight one another by day, but at night they show profound similarity in their dreams and myths. The agreement is too profound to be produced by chance alone. It is therefore attributed to a similarity of the psyche at the deepest layers of the unconscious. These similar-appearing symbolic images are termed archetypes.

The OCAI captures the underlying structure of these psychological archetypes in its core dimensions. That is, assessing organizational culture using the Competing Values Framework taps into the fundamental organizing framework used by people when they obtain, interpret, and draw conclusions about information (see Cameron and Ettington, 1988, for a more thorough explanation of the basis of this claim). Research has found that individuals describe the cultures of their organizations according to this psychological archetype, and cultural information is interpreted by individuals in the context of their underlying archetype. The manner in which organizational culture is naturally interpreted, in other words, is congruent with the dimensions of the Competing Values Framework (see Mason and Mitroff, 1973; Mitroff and Kilmann, 1978). The key to assessing organizational culture, therefore, is to identify aspects of the organization that reflect key values and assumptions in the organization and then to give individuals an opportunity to respond using their underlying archetypal framework. The OCAI allows this to occur.

Six content dimensions serve as the basis for the OCAI:

1. The dominant characteristics of the organization, or what the overall organization is like

2. The leadership style and approach that permeate the organization

3. The management of employees or the style that characterizes how employees are treated and what the working environment is like

4. The organizational glue or bonding mechanisms that hold the organization together

5. The strategic emphases that define what areas of emphasis drive the organization's strategy

6. The criteria of success that determine how victory is defined and what gets rewarded and celebrated

In combination, these content dimensions reflect fundamental cultural values and implicit assumptions about the way the organization functions. They reflect "how things are" in the organization. This list of six content dimensions is not comprehensive, of course, but it has proved in past research to provide an adequate picture of the type of culture that exists in an organization. Therefore, by having organization members respond to questions about these dimensions, the underlying organizational culture can be uncovered. Again, this is especially true because the core structure of the competing values model is consistent with the dominant psychological archetype, and respondents are able to use a structure that is familiar to them to reflect their cultural ratings.

In reference to the pattern dimensions of organizational culture, the literature has been filled with a wide variety of such dimensions. Cameron and Ettington (1988) report more than twenty, including dimensions such as internal-external focus, speed, riskiness, participativeness, clarity, power distance, masculinity, and individualism. Each of these dimensions helps establish a profile or a pattern for an organization's culture. However, by far the three most dominant and most frequently appearing pattern dimensions in the literature are *cultural strength, cultural congruence,* and *cultural type.* Cultural strength refers to the power or preeminence of the culture in affecting what happens in an organization. For example, Deal and Kennedy (1982, p. 5) asserted that "a strong culture has almost always been the driving force behind the continuing success in American business." Cultural congruence refers to the extent to which the culture reflected in one part of the organization is similar to and consistent with the culture reflected in another part of the organization: For example, Nadler and Tushman (1980, p. 275) found that "other things being equal, the greater the total degree of congruence or fit between the various components [of an organization], the more effective will be organizational behavior at multiple levels." Cultural type refers to the specific kind of culture that is reflected in the organization (for example, an innovative, risk-oriented culture). Cameron and Ettington (1988, p. 385) found that "the effectiveness of organizations is more closely associated with the type of culture present than with the congruence or the strength of that culture." Kotter and Heskett (1992) found that the major differentiating factor between high-performing companies (American Airlines, Bankers Trust, Anheuser-Busch, PepsiCo, Hewlett-Packard, Con-Agra, Shell, Albertsons, Dayton Hudson, Wal-Mart, Golden West, Springs Industries) and a matched set of lower-performing companies (Northwest Airlines, Citicorp, Coors, Xerox, Archer Daniels Midland, Texaco, Winn-Dixie, J. C. Penney, H. F. Ahmanson, Fieldcrest Cannon) was the strength, congruence (culture aligned with strategy), and type of culture (firms that valued equally customers, stockholders, and employees).

The OCAI is unique in its ability to identify the organization's cultural strength, congruence, and type. As discussed earlier, by observing the overall cultural profile of an organization, we can immediately detect the extent to which one or more cultures are strong (or dominant) in that organization. By reviewing the profiles associated with each of the six scenarios (questions) individually, we can detect the extent to which the six profiles are congruent with one another or are heterogeneous (incongruent). Finally, the culture profiles make it easy to tell what type of culture the organization possesses based on the quadrant that receives the most emphasis. Our own research on hundreds of organizations has shown that clan and hierarchy cultures appear more frequently in organizations than market or adhocracy cultures.

Reliability and Validity of the OCAI

Of course, for the OCAI to be useful, we need to be confident that it is both reliable and valid. We need to have evidence that it measures what it says it measures and that it does so every time we administer the instrument. Fortunately, the instrument has been used by numerous researchers in studies of many different types of organizations. These studies have all tested the reliability and validity of the instrument in the course of their analyses. Several of these studies are briefly summarized here to provide evidence of the reliability and validity of both the instrument and the approach.

Reliability

Reliability refers to the extent to which the instrument measures culture types consistently. That is, do the different items that purport to assess a culture type really assess it? One study that tested the reliability of the OCAI was conducted by Quinn and Spreitzer (1991) in which 796 executives from eighty-six different public utility firms rated their own organization's culture. They included top managers (13 percent of the sample), upper-middle managers

(45 percent), middle managers (39 percent), and line and staff workers (2 percent). Cronbach alpha coefficients (a reliability statistic) were computed for each of the culture types being assessed by the instrument. Each coefficient was statistically significant and very satisfactory compared to normal standards of reliability. Coefficients were .74 for the clan culture, .79 for the adhocracy culture, .73 for the hierarchy culture, and .71 for the market culture. In other words, respondents tended to rate their organization's culture consistently across the various questions on the instrument.

Yeung, Brockbank, and Ulrich (1991) also provided evidence of reliability in their study of 10,300 executives in 1,064 businesses. These businesses included many of the corporations on the list of Fortune 500 companies. The key respondents were human resource executives and various associates that these executives selected to complete the assessment instrument. The number of respondents averaged nine per business. The OCAI was used to gather data on the culture of each of these organizations. The various question alternatives were grouped together into the appropriate culture types, and reliability coefficients were computed. The results showed that the clan culture reliability was .79, the adhocracy culture reliability was .80, the hierarchy culture reliability was .76, and the market culture reliability was .77. In each case, reliability coefficients exceeded satisfactory levels. Parenthetically, Yeung and colleagues found that the largest percentage of firms were dominated by the hierarchy culture (44 percent), clan and adhocracy cultures were next (15 and 14 percent, respectively), and surprisingly, no firms were dominated by the market quadrant. All had moderate emphasis on the market culture type. Six percent of the firms had all the cultures equally dominant, and 22 percent had no culture emerge as dominant.

Zammuto and Krakower (1991) used this instrument to investigate the culture of higher education institutions. More than thirteen hundred respondents, including administrators (39 percent of the sample), department chairpersons (34 percent), and trustees (27 percent), rated the culture of their organizations, resulting in reliability coefficients of .82 for clan reliability, .83 for adhocracy reliability, .78 for market reliability, and .67 for hierarchy reliability.

Numerous additional studies can be cited (see, for example, Peterson, Cameron, Spencer, and White, 1991), but in every case that we know of, the reliability of these culture types has shown patterns consistent with those reported here. In other words, sufficient evidence has been produced regarding the reliability of the OCAI to create confidence that it matches or exceeds the reliability of the most commonly used instruments in the social and organizational sciences.

Validity

Validity refers to the extent to which phenomena that are supposed to be measured are actually measured. That is, does this instrument really measure four types of organizational culture? Cameron and Freeman (1991) produced evidence for the validity of the OCAI in their study of organizational culture in 334 institutions of higher education. This sample of organizations is representative of the entire population of four-year colleges and universities in the United States. In each of these institutions, individuals were identified who could provide an overall institutional perspective so that in each institution respondents included the president, the chief academic, finance, student affairs, external affairs, and institutional research officers, selected department heads, and selected members of the board of trustees. From 12 to 20 individuals responded at each institution, and a total of 3,406 individuals participated.

No organization was characterized totally by only one culture, but dominant cultures were clearly evident in most institutions. The most frequently appearing culture was a clan culture, and the least frequently appearing culture was a market culture. A total of 236 institutions had congruent cultures (that is, one culture type dominated most aspects of the organization), whereas 98 had incongruent cultures (the culture type was not consistent across various aspects of the organization).

An examination was made of the relationships between three dimensions of culture—cultural strength, congruence, and type—and organizational effectiveness. In previous research, Cameron had identified dimensions of organizational effectiveness in institutions of higher education, and this study used those dimensions to investigate the extent to which strong cultures were more effective than weak cultures, congruent cultures were more effective than incongruent cultures, and effectiveness differed among the various types of organizational cultures. The study found that cultural strength and cultural congruence were not nearly as powerful in predicting organizational effectiveness as culture type. That is, no statistically significant differences existed between strong and weak cultures and between congruent and incongruent cultures and various dimensions of organizational effectiveness, but significant differences did exist when comparing the various culture types.

Evidence for the validity of the culture instrument was uncovered when the culture type was matched with the domain of effectiveness in which the organization excelled and by the type of decision making, structure, and strategy employed. Institutions that had clan-type cultures were most effective in domains of performance relating to morale, satisfaction, internal communication, and supportiveness, all attributes consistent with clan values. Institutions that had an adhocracy-type culture were most effective in domains of performance relating to adaptation, system openness, innovation, and cutting-edge knowledge—all attributes consistent with adhocracy values. Institutions that had a market-type culture were most effective in domains of performance relating to their ability to acquire needed resources such as revenues, good faculty, institutional visibility, and so forth—all attributes consistent with a market culture. Institutions with hierarchy cultures did not excel in any of the performance domains.

Additional statistical analyses revealed that institutions with different types of cultures also had different kinds of organizational strategies, decision processes, and structures. Clan cultures were characterized by high cohesion, collegiality in decision making, and a special sense of institutional identity and mission. Adhocracy cultures were characterized by innovation, aggressive strategies, increasing boundary spanning, and initiative. Market cultures were characterized by aggressiveness and prospector strategies. Hierarchy cultures were characterized by tight financial control and efficiency. In brief, these analyses produced results that are highly consistent with the espoused values and organizational attributes claimed to be typical of each culture type in the Competing Values Framework. In other words, strong evidence for concurrent validity was produced.

Quinn and Spreitzer (1991) also found evidence for two additional kinds of validity—convergent validity and discriminant validity. Tests for these two types of validity were conducted using a multitrait-multimethod analysis and a multidimensional scaling analysis.

The multitrait-multimethod analysis was produced by using two different instruments to assess organizational culture. One instrument was the OCAI being explained here. The other instrument assessed the same cultural dimensions using a different response scale, a Likert-type scale where each alternative scenario was rated from 1 to 5. The scales of the four culture quadrants represented the four traits, and the two different instruments represented the two methods. The goal of the analysis was to determine if the variance explained between the four traits (the four cultures) exceeded the variance accounted for by the method used (the two different instruments). To produce evidence of validity, correlation coefficients in the same culture quadrant should be significantly different from zero and of moderate magnitude (Campbell and Fisk, 1959). Convergent validity was supported, as it turned out, when the multitrait-multimethod correlation matrix was examined. As required, all diagonal correlation coefficients were statistically different from zero ($p < .001$), and they ranged between .212 and .515, a moderate level of correlation.

Discriminant validity was tested in three ways. In the first test, scales in the same culture quadrant were tested to see if they correlated higher with each other than they did with scales of different culture quadrants measured by separate instruments (Campbell and Fisk, 1959). Twenty-three out of the twenty-four comparisons were consistent with expectations, providing solid support for discriminant validity. In the second test, scales in the same culture were expected to correlate higher with each other than with scales in a different culture quadrant measured by the same method (Campbell and Fisk, 1959). In sixteen of the twenty-four scales, this was the case, providing moderate support for discriminant validity. In the third test, the same pattern of interrelationships was expected to exist within and between each of the independent methods (Campbell and Fisk, 1959). Kendall's coefficient of concordance was computed, which produced a coefficient of .764 ($p < .001$), indicating strong support for discriminant validity. In other words, these three tests using the multitrait-multimethod procedure provided support for both convergent and discriminant validity of the model and the instrument.

The multidimensional scaling procedure also produced strong support for convergent and discriminant validity. Figure A.1 shows the positioning of each culture type when measured with two different types of instruments. Guttman and Lingoes's coefficient of alienation ($r = .076$) and Shepherd and Kruskal's stress coefficient (stress = .056) indicate a satisfactory fit of the data to the model (see Kruskal and Wish, 1978). Moreover, it can be seen from the figure that each culture type appears in the appropriate quadrant, that like cultures are positioned closer to each other than to unlike culture types, and that each culture type is positioned in a different quadrant. In other words, strong support is provided for convergent and discriminant validity using this multidimensional scaling technique.

Further evidence of validity was produced by Zammuto and Krakower (1991). In their study of college cultures, they found that clan cultures were strongly associated with decentralization, trust, a sense of equity among organization members, high morale, and satisfaction with the leader. All of these factors are consistent with the core values represented by the clan culture. They found that adhoc-

Figure A.1 Multidimensional Scaling Results of the Competing Values Dimensions

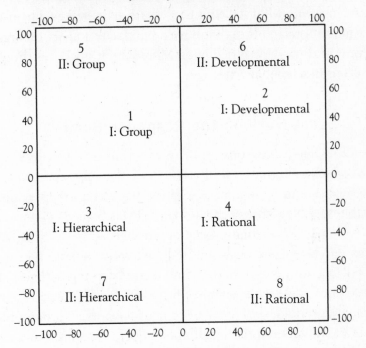

Shepherd and Kruskal's Stress Coefficient = .056
Guttman and Lingoes's Coefficient of Alienation = .076

racy cultures were strongly associated with formality, propensity toward change, and a proactive orientation toward strategy and improvement—all perfectly consistent with espoused adhocratic culture values. The market culture was strongly associated with directive leadership, confrontation and conflict, reward for achievement, and strong directives—all compatible with the market culture values. The hierarchy culture was strongly associated with formalization, resistance to change, stability, a reactive orientation toward change, and low morale—again, largely consistent with these organizational attributes.

Additional studies have also examined the validity of the OCAI, but as was the case with reliability tests, we know of no study where contradictory disconfirmatory evidence has been produced. In other words, the empirical evidence suggests that the OCAI measures what it claims to measure, namely, key dimensions of organizational culture that have a significant impact on organizational and individual behavior. Moreover, it measures these dimensions in a reliable way.

A Note on the Response Scale

The OCAI uses a response scale in which individuals divide 100 points among alternatives. This is known as an *ipsative rating scale*. The most common alternative rating scale is a Likert scale, in which respondents rate each alternative in each question on a scale of 1 to 5 or 1 to 7—ranging, say, from strongly agree to strongly disagree. We have consciously selected the ipsative alternative for the OCAI, but we have done research using both types of response scales. The OCAI scale has advantages and disadvantages of which researchers should be aware. The primary advantage is that it highlights and differentiates the cultural uniqueness that actually exists in organizations. That is, the OCAI provides a 100-point scale for rating instead of a 5- or 7-point scale using a Likert format. That results in more differentiation in ratings. A second major advantage is that respondents are forced to identify the trade-offs that actually exist in the organization. When the Likert scale is used, respondents tend to rate all quadrants high or all quadrants low. Less differentiation occurs.

On the other hand, ipsative response scales do not produce independent responses. The response to alternative A in question 1, for example, is related to the response to alternative B in question 1. In a Likert format, each response is assumed to be independent. Normal correlational statistical analyses, which are based on the assumption of independent responses on each item, are usually not appropriate for analyzing this kind of data. However, Cameron and Freeman (1991) and Zammuto and Krakower (1991) have reviewed arguments for the appropriateness of some standard statistical techniques for these kinds of data, and examples of alternative statistical techniques are available in those articles. On the other hand, Quinn and Spreitzer (1991) and Yeung, Brockbank, and Ulrich (1991) are among the researchers who used a Likert response scale and analyzed the culture data using standard statistical procedures.

For research purposes, we suggest that scholars select the statistical technique that best matches their research agendas and central research questions. We will be pleased to discuss with researchers the different statistical alternatives available and to learn how the instrument is being used in others' research projects.

Appendix B
Psychometric Analyses of
the Management Skills
Assessment Instrument (MSAI)

Because the Management Skills Assessment Instrument (MSAI) has been widely used and is such an important supplement to organizational culture change efforts—as well as being an excellent personal management improvement tool—a brief discussion of its psychometric properties is included here. This discussion may be helpful to individuals who want to use this instrument in their own organization change efforts or for research purposes. The MSAI itself is reproduced at the end of this appendix.

The best and most sophisticated analysis of the psychometric properties of the MSAI was conducted by Lee Collett and Carlos Mora at the University of Michigan. The key question being addressed was this: Does the MSAI measure management skills that match the Competing Values Framework? That is, do management skills in one quadrant have the predicted relationships to management skills in the other quadrants? Does the theoretical framework accurately map the MSAI?

To address this issue, Collett and Mora (1996) developed a new statistical technique called a *Within-Person Deviation Score* or *D-Score*. They used a subset of the 40,000-person data set that has been gathered on the MSAI. Their analysis consisted of 8,816 cases. Because of their selection procedures, there is no reason to expect that the subset they analyzed differed in any systematic way from the total data set. Collett and Mora used linear combinations (means) of scores on the items comprising each competency area (such as managing teams or managing innovation) so that from the original sixty items they produced twelve competency dimension scores and four quadrant scores. Analyses were conducted first on responses of individual subordinates and then on aggregated responses consisting of the average item scores of all individuals who rated the same manager. Three correlation matrices were computed: (1) correlations among the four quadrant indices were computed to check on the hypothesized relationships among adjacent and diagonal quadrants; (2) a 12-by-16 matrix of correlations among the twelve competency dimension scores was computed to compare intraquadrant and interquadrant relationships; and (3) a 12-by-60 matrix of correlations was computed (twelve competency dimensions and sixty items) to compare intracompetency dimension correlations (reliabilities) with intercompetency dimension correlations.

The results of these analyses are reported in the section that follows an explanation of the D-Score statistical procedure.

The Within-Person D-Score

Collett and Mora developed a new statistical technique for analyzing the MSAI data because, they reasoned, the ratings of individuals who assess the management behavior of another manager do not follow the normal statistical assumptions. Ordinarily it is assumed that a set of ratings of any phenomenon will array itself around a normal curve. However, when a manager is being rated by a single subordinate, for example, those ratings are unlikely to be arrayed on a normal curve. They constitute a repeated measure of the same phenomenon. Those ratings, therefore, are likely to be affected by a set of factors that add bias to the ratings, most notably the behavior of the manager and the personal biases of the rater. The idea behind the Within-Person D-Scores, therefore, came from the basic theory of repeated measures analysis of variance, which depicts individuals' scores as a linear combination of additive influences. A person's rating (X) on an MSAI item is likely to consist of seven additive components. These can be depicted mathematically as follows:

$$X_{ijkm} = \mu + M_m + (O_{i(m)} + C_m + Q) = F_k + E_{j(ikm)}$$

where

μ is the mean performance by the population of managers on the competencies being measured.

M_m is the amount that the actual performance of manager m is above or below μ.

$O_{i(m)}$ is the observational error (+ or −) of person i in rating the performance of manager m. The parentheses in the subscript indicate nesting; that is, persons are nested within managers (m) in that each person rates only one manager. It is assumed that this component is randomly distributed about a mean of zero.

C_m is the bias (+ or −) caused by the personal charisma of manager m. It is assumed that managers providing the data are likely to be among the best performers in their organizations; hence most managers have positive m scores with the occasional low scores producing a distribution with a strong negative skew.

Q is the biasing effect (+ or −) of the questionnaire and administration procedures. In the case of the MSAI, the use of all positively worded items probably produces a uniform positive influence.

F_k is the actual influence (+ or −) of dimension k on the scores of each item in the dimension.

$E_{j(ikm)}$ is the error (+ or −) of person i rating manager m on item j in dimension k. Again, the parentheses in the subscript indicates that items are nested within persons, dimensions, and managers.

The parentheses around the O, C, and Q terms indicate that these three sources of bias are confounded in the average response of each person—they are person effects. Their combined effects tend to be larger than the other elements in the equation, and their combined effects will be positively biased, thus pushing raw scores on each item toward the top end of the response scale. The distribution of scores, therefore, will have a strong negative skew. The challenge is to eliminate the influence of O, C, and Q (the person) so that the effects of M and F (the behaviors of the manager) are able to be detected. This is done by computing a mean score (average of the sixty items) for each person and then partitioning deviations around this grand mean into a within-person component and a between-person component. In a repeated-measures ANOVA, these deviations are squared and summed to obtain sums of squares and variances for each component. However, in this analysis, the deviation scores themselves were used. The deviation score (D-Score) was computed for each of the sixty items by subtracting the mean score for an individual respondent from the original score for that item. Dimension and quadrant scores were computed by averaging the items together that were theorized to fit within the appropriate dimension and quadrant. Correlations among item, dimension, and quadrant D-Scores were then computed.

Characteristics of D-Scores

D-Scores are ipsative scores in that they sum to zero. This means that each high positive item score must be counterbalanced by a negative score of equal size. Thus an item D-Score tends to have a built-in negative correlation with most other items. The expected value of correlations among ipsative scales is negative; hence positive correlations (.50 or higher) between same-dimension items or same-quadrant items, coupled with negative correlations between diagonal-quadrant dimensions and quadrants, provide strong support for the validity of the MSAI. For ipsative scales, moderate negative correlations would be predicted for dimensions in adjacent quadrants.

It should also be pointed out that D-Scores have eliminated the person effect (O, C, Q). An original score pattern of 444454 . . . 4 on various items yields the same D-Score as a score pattern of 111121 . . . 1. The D-Score represents only the relative position of the score within a set of scores for an individual rater. The results of a D-Score analysis, then, show the variance within a person's own response pattern, not the variance across different raters' response patterns, as in normal statistical analyses. To determine if the MSAI is valid and useful, we are interested in the ratings of individuals as they rate their own manager, not as multiple raters rate multiple managers. The research questions, then, are the following:

Are adhocracy quadrant skills negatively correlated with hierarchy quadrant skills, as predicted by the framework?

Are clan and market quadrants negatively correlated?

Are the competency dimensions within each quadrant positively correlated?

Do intradimension item correlations show adequate reliability?

Results of the Analyses

Quadrant-to-Quadrant Correlations

Figure B.1 reports the results of the correlations among the quadrants. It shows that, consistent with the Competing Values Framework, the correlation between the clan and market quadrants is –.43, and the correlation between the adhocracy and hierarchy quadrants is –.68. As expected, the correlations between adjacent quadrants are negative, but the coefficients are much smaller than between diagonal quadrants (adhocracy to market, –.10; market to hierarchy, –.18; clan to hierarchy, –.34; clan to adhocracy, –.23).

Dimension-to-Dimension Correlations

Dimensions within a quadrant should have positive or very slightly negative correlations among themselves to be consistent with the Competing Values Framework. The results of the analysis, shown in Table B.1, confirm this prediction. The dimensions in the clan quadrant have positive intercorrelations with one another and strong negative correlations with the market quadrant dimensions. Correlations with dimensions in adjacent quadrants are positive or

Figure B.1 D-Score Correlations Among Quadrants

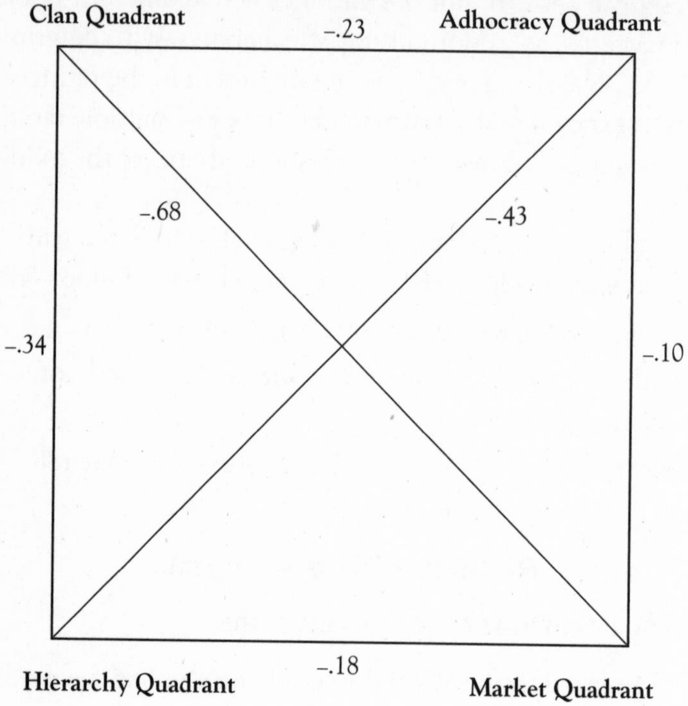

slightly negative, and in only one case (managing the control system) is the correlation more negative than the diagonal quadrant correlations. In seventeen of eighteen instances, the theorized adjacent-quadrant relationship holds for the clan quadrant.

The correlations among dimensions in the adhocracy quadrant are near zero, some slightly positive and some slightly negative. In sixteen of eighteen instances, they are lower than the diagonal quadrant correlations. The theorized adjacent-quadrant correlations hold in twelve of eighteen cases.

The intramarket quadrant correlations are also mainly positive, confirming the within-quadrant relationships among dimensions. The theorized diagonal-quadrant relationships hold in all cases and in fifteen of eighteen cases in the adjacent-quadrant relationships.

Table B.1 D-Score Correlations Among Dimensions

	T	IR	DO	I	F	CI	C	E	CS	A	Con	Coor
Clan												
Managing teams (T)		+.55	+.18	+.09	–.20	–.22	–.61	–.42	–.26	–.05	–.32	–.03
Managing interpersonal relationships (IR)			+.22	+.12	–.33	–.19	–.64	–.46	–.19	–.10	–.33	–.01
Managing the development of others (DO)				+.10	–.15	–.01	–.40	–.17	–.30	–.00	–.30	–.21
Adhocracy												
Managing innovation (I)					+.03	+.04	–.41	–.11	–.22	–.32	–.33	–.16
Managing the future (F)						–.06	–.03	+.56	–.11	–.09	–.11	–.15
Managing continuous improvements (CI)							–.04	+.02	–.08	–.11	–.01	–.16
Market												
Managing competitiveness (C)								+.63	+.50	+.24	+.30	–.16
Energizing employees (E)									–.01	–.14	+.06	–.25
Managing customer service (CS)										–.07	–.02	+.05
Hierarchy												
Managing acculturation (A)											+.13	+.04
Managing the control system (Con)												+.14
Managing coordination (Coor)												

The dimensions in the hierarchy quadrant are also near zero and all slightly positive, confirming their reliability (inasmuch as the expected relationship is slightly negative). The theorized diagonal-quadrant relationships are confirmed, although with less strong results than in the other quadrants, and the adjacent-quadrant results are consistent with predictions in eleven of eighteen instances. Whereas the results for the hierarchy quadrant are less strong than for the other quadrants, the diagonal-quadrant results are consistent with theorized relationships, and the results for adjacent-quadrant relationships are largely confirmed (with a few exceptions).

Item Dimension Correlations

An examination of the correlations with each item and the other items in its theorized dimension (within-dimension correlations) compared to the correlations between each item and the other three dimensions (outside-dimension correlations) reveals that every competency dimension has strong reliabilities (well above .50, a very strong reliability using ipsative measures). Two items on the survey—numbers 31 and 60—appear to be rather weak measures of their theorized dimensions, and eliminating them from the MSAI would strengthen the psychometric power of the questionnaire. On the other hand, they are items that assess important aspects of a manager's behavior, and although not strongly correlated with other items on the survey, they are important aspects of a successful manager's behavior.

In sum, these analyses provide strong support for the MSAI as an instrument that can assist the culture change process. It maps very well the relationships among quadrants and competency dimensions theorized by the Competing Values Framework. The critical management skills being assessed by the instrument possess the same theorized relationships to one another as the culture quadrants. It may be used with some confidence, then, in helping managers develop competencies that will foster culture change in desired directions.

Management Skills Assessment Instrument
Self-Assessment Form

This instrument is designed to obtain descriptions of your management behavior on the job. There are no right or wrong answers. The items on the questionnaire have been derived from research on managerial behavior, and their intent is to provide you with a profile of your own managerial competencies. The items do not assess your style; they assess your behavior. Therefore, you should respond on the basis of what you do, not what you think you should do.

Your responses will be compared to the responses you receive from subordinates, peers, and superiors in your organization. This information will be compiled and provided to you in a personalized feedback report. You will also be able to compare your competencies profile with those of eighty thousand other managers.

A standardized answer sheet has been provided for your responses. Please mark your answers on that sheet. This will facilitate entry of the data into a computer so your feedback report can be prepared. Do not use the questionnaire itself for your answers.

You have been assigned a number for data analysis purposes. This number should already be printed on your answer sheet. Please make no other marks on the answer sheet except your responses to each question and your name.

The questionnaire should take about thirty minutes to complete. When you finish, fax your answer sheet back to Behavioral Data Services by (*date*). You need not fax back the pages of the questionnaire itself.

Thank you very much for your cooperation.

Management Skills Survey
Self-Rating Form

Describe your behavior as a manager. Respond to the items as you actually behave most of the time, not as you would like to behave. If you are unsure of an answer, make your best guess. Please mark your answers on the answer sheet. Use the following scale in your ratings:

5—Strongly Agree

4—Moderately Agree

3—Slightly Agree and/or Slightly Disagree

2—Moderately Disagree

1—Strongly Disagree

	Strongly Agree	Moderately Agre	Slightly Agree and/or Slightly Disagree	Moderately Disagree	Strongly Disagree
1. I communicate in a supportive way when people in my unit share their problems with me.	5	4	3	2	1
2. I encourage others in my unit to generate new ideas and methods.	5	4	3	2	1
3. I motivate and energize others to do a better job.	5	4	3	2	1
4. I keep close track of how my unit is performing.	5	4	3	2	1
5. I regularly coach subordinates to improve their management skills so they can achieve higher levels of performance.	5	4	3	2	1
6. I insist on intense hard work and high productivity from my subordinates.	5	4	3	2	1
7. I establish ambitious goals that challenge subordinates to achieve performance levels above the standard.	5	4	3	2	1
8. I generate, or help others obtain, the resources necessary to implement their innovative ideas.	5	4	3	2	1

	Strongly Agree	Moderately Agree	Slightly Agree and/or Slightly Disagree	Moderately Disagree	Strongly Disagree
9. When someone comes up with a new idea, I help sponsor them to follow through on it.	5	4	3	2	1
10. I make certain that all employees are clear about our policies, values, and objectives.	5	4	3	2	1
11. I make certain that others have a clear picture of how their job fits with others in the organization.	5	4	3	2	1
12. I build cohesive, committed teams of people.	5	4	3	2	1
13. I give my subordinates regular feedback about how I think they're doing.	5	4	3	2	1
14. I articulate a clear vision of what can be accomplished in the future.	5	4	3	2	1
15. I foster a sense of competitiveness that helps members of my work group perform at higher levels than members of other units.	5	4	3	2	1
16. I assure that regular reports and assessments occur in my unit.	5	4	3	2	1
17. I interpret and simplify complex information so that it makes sense to others and can be shared throughout the organization.	5	4	3	2	1
18. I facilitate effective information sharing and problem solving in my group.	5	4	3	2	1
19. I foster rational, systematic decision analysis in my unit (e.g., logically analyzing component parts of problems) to reduce the complexity of important issues.	5	4	3	2	1
20. I make sure that others in my unit are provided with opportunities for personal growth and development.	5	4	3	2	1

	Strongly Agree	Moderately Agree	Slightly Agree and/or Slightly Disagree	Moderately Disagree	Strongly Disagree
21. I create an environment where involvement and participation in decisions are encouraged and rewarded.	5	4	3	2	1
22. In groups I lead, I make sure that sufficient attention is given to both task accomplishment and interpersonal relationships.	5	4	3	2	1
23. When giving negative feedback to others, I foster their self-improvement rather than defensiveness or anger.	5	4	3	2	1
24. I give others assignments and responsibilities that provide opportunities for their personal growth and development.	5	4	3	2	1
25. I actively help prepare others to move up in the organization.	5	4	3	2	1
26. I regularly come up with new, creative ideas regarding processes, products, or procedures for my organization.	5	4	3	2	1
27. I constantly restate and reinforce my vision of the future to members of my unit.	5	4	3	2	1
28. I help others visualize a new kind of future that includes possibilities as well as probabilities.	5	4	3	2	1
29. I am always working to improve the processes we use to achieve our desired output.	5	4	3	2	1
30. I push my unit to achieve world-class competitive performance in service and/or products.	5	4	3	2	1
31. By empowering others in my unit, I foster a motivational climate that energizes everyone involved.	5	4	3	2	1

	Strongly Agree	Moderately Agree	Slightly Agree and/or Slightly Disagree	Moderately Disagree	Strongly Disagree
32. I have consistent and frequent personal contact with my internal and my external customers.	5	4	3	2	1
33. I make sure that we assess how well we are meeting our customers' expectations.	5	4	3	2	1
34. I provide experiences for employees that help them become socialized and integrated into the culture of our organization.	5	4	3	2	1
35. I increase the competitiveness of my unit by encouraging others to provide services and/or products that surprise and delight customers by exceeding their expectations.	5	4	3	2	1
36. I have established a control system that assures consistency in quality, service, cost, and productivity in my unit.	5	4	3	2	1
37. I coordinate regularly with managers in other units in my organization.	5	4	3	2	1
38. I routinely share information across functional boundaries in my organization to facilitate coordination.	5	4	3	2	1
39. I use a measurement system that consistently monitors both work processes and outcomes.	5	4	3	2	1
40. I clarify for members of my unit exactly what is expected of them.	5	4	3	2	1
41. I assure that everything we do is focused on better serving our customers.	5	4	3	2	1
42. I facilitate a climate of aggressiveness and intensity in my unit.	5	4	3	2	1

	Strongly Agree	Moderately Agree	Slightly Agree and/or Slightly Disagree	Moderately Disagree	Strongly Disagree
43. I constantly monitor the strengths and weaknesses of our best competition and provide my unit with information on how we measure up.	5	4	3	2	1
44. I facilitate a climate of continuous improvement in my unit.	5	4	3	2	1
45. I have developed a clear strategy for helping my unit successfully accomplish my vision of the future.	5	4	3	2	1
46. I capture the imagination and emotional commitment of others when I talk about my vision of the future.	5	4	3	2	1
47. I facilitate a work environment where peers as well as subordinates learn from and help develop one another.	5	4	3	2	1
48. I listen openly and attentively to others who give me their ideas, even when I disagree.	5	4	3	2	1
49. When leading a group, I ensure collaboration and positive conflict resolution among group members.	5	4	3	2	1
50. I foster trust and openness by showing understanding for the point of view of individuals who come to me with problems or concerns.	5	4	3	2	1
51. I create an environment where experimentation and creativity are rewarded and recognized.	5	4	3	2	1
52. I encourage everyone in my unit to constantly improve and update everything they do.	5	4	3	2	1
53. I encourage all employees to make small improvements continuously in the way they do their jobs.	5	4	3	2	1
54. I make sure that my unit continually gathers information on our customers' needs and preferences.	5	4	3	2	1

	Strongly Agree	Moderately Agree	Slightly Agree and/or Slightly Disagree	Moderately Disagree	Strongly Disagree
55. I involve customers in my unit's planning and evaluations.	5	4	3	2	1
56. I establish ceremonies and rewards in my unit that reinforce the values and culture of our organization.	5	4	3	2	1
57. I maintain a formal system for gathering and responding to information that originates in other units outside my own.	5	4	3	2	1
58. I initiate cross-functional teams or task forces that focus on important organizational issues.	5	4	3	2	1
59. I help my employees strive for improvement in all aspects of their lives, not just in job-related activities.	5	4	3	2	1
60. I create a climate where individuals in my unit want to achieve higher levels of performance than the competition.	5	4	3	2	1

Managerial Effectiveness
Self-Rating Form

For questions 61–73, please rate your effectiveness in performing these skills. Use the following scale in your rating:

5—Outstanding

4—Very Good

3—Average

2—Marginal

1—Poor

	Outstanding	Very Good	Average	Marginal	Poor
61. Managing teams (building effective, cohesive, smooth-functioning teams)	5	4	3	2	1
62. Managing interpersonal relationships (listening to and providing supportive feedback to others)	5	4	3	2	1
63. Managing the development of others (helping others improve their performance and obtain personal development opportunities)	5	4	3	2	1
64. Fostering innovation (encouraging others to innovate and generate new ideas)	5	4	3	2	1
65. Managing the future (communicating a clear vision of the future and facilitating its accomplishment)	5	4	3	2	1
66. Managing continuous improvement (fostering an orientation toward continuous improvement among employees in everything they do)	5	4	3	2	1
67. Managing competitiveness (fostering an aggressive orientation toward exceeding competitors' performance)	5	4	3	2	1
68. Energizing employees (motivating others to put forth extra effort and to work aggressively)	5	4	3	2	1
69. Managing customer service (fostering a focus on service and involvement with customers)	5	4	3	2	1
70. Managing acculturation (helping others become clear about what is expected of them and about organizational culture and standards)	5	4	3	2	1

	Outstanding	Very Good	Average	Marginal	Poor
71. Managing the control system (having measurement and monitoring systems in place to keep close track of processes and performance)	5	4	3	2	1
72. Managing coordination (sharing information across functional boundaries and fostering coordination with other units)	5	4	3	2	1
73. Overall management competency (general level of managerial ability)	5	4	3	2	1

74. On the basis of your level of management competency, how high in the organization do you expect to go in your career? (CHECK ONLY ONE ALTERNATIVE)

   5—To the very top of the organization

   4—Near the top—just below the CEO

   3—To a senior position—perhaps member of the executive committee

   2—One level above where you are now

   1—No higher than the current position

75. Compared to all other managers you've known, how would you rate your own competency as a manager of managers?

   5—Top 5%

   4—Top 10%

   3—Top 25%

   2—Top 50 %

   1—In the bottom half

Importance Information

Note: The scale changes for question 76–87. Please read carefully. In order to succeed in your current position, how important is each of the following skills? Use the following scale in your rating:

5—Critically Important

4—Very Important

3—Moderately Important

2—Of Some Importance

1—Of Little Importance

	Critically Important	Very Important	Moderately Important	Of Some Importance	Of Little Importance
76. Managing teams (building effective, cohesive, smooth-functioning teams)	5	4	3	2	1
77. Managing interpersonal relationships (listening to and providing supportive feedback to others)	5	4	3	2	1
78. Managing the development of others (helping others improve their performance and obtain personal development opportunities)	5	4	3	2	1
79. Fostering innovation (encouraging others to innovate and generate new ideas)	5	4	3	2	1
80. Managing the future (communicating a clear vision of the future and facilitating its accomplishment)	5	4	3	2	1
81. Managing continuous improvement (fostering an orientation toward continuous improvement among employees in everything they do)	5	4	3	2	1
82. Managing competitiveness (fostering an aggressive orientation toward exceeding competitors' performance)	5	4	3	2	1
83. Energizing employees (motivating others to put forth extra effort and to work aggressively)	5	4	3	2	1
84. Managing customer service (fostering a focus on service and involvement with customers)	5	4	3	2	1

	Critically Important	Very Important	Moderately Important	Of Some Importance	Of Little Importance
85. Managing acculturation (helping others become clear about what is expected of them and about organizational culture and standards)	5	4	3	2	1
86. Managing the control system (having measurement and monitoring systems in place to keep close track of processes and performance)	5	4	3	2	1
87. Managing coordination (sharing information across functional boundaries and fostering coordination with other units)	5	4	3	2	1

Demographic Information

In order to provide comparative feedback, please provide the following information about yourself. Mark your answers in the box located in the bottom right corner of your answer sheet, titled "Demographic Information."

1. _____ Person completing the survey (Who are you?)
    (1) Participant attending program
    (2) Subordinate to participant
    (3) Peer of participant
    (4) Superior of participant
    (5) Superior 2 or more levels above participant

2. _____ Sex
    (1) Female
    (2) Male

3. _____ Age
    (1) 30 or under   (5) 46–50
    (2) 31–35   (6) 51–55
    (3) 36–40   (7) 56–60
    (4) 41–45   (8) 61 or over

4. _____ Job title
    (1) Vice President
    (2) General Manager
    (3) Director
    (4) Functional Manager
    (5) Superintendent
    (6) Assistant Manager
    (7) Plant Manager
    (8) Coordinator/Supervisor/Administrator
    (9) Other

5. _____ Work location
    (1) Corporate
    (2) Division
    (3) Plant
    (4) Region/Zone
    (5) Other

6. _____ Number of subordinates reporting *directly* to you

    (1) 0   (5) 10–12

    (2) 1–3   (6) 13–15

    (3) 4–6   (7) 16–18

    (4) 7–9   (8) 19+

7. _____ Number of promotions within the last five years

    (1) 1   (6) 6

    (2) 2   (7) 7

    (3) 3   (8) 8 or more

    (4) 4   (9) 0

    (5) 5

8. _____ Percent increase received over least year's base salary

    (1) 0%   (6) 13%–15%

    (2) 1%–3%   (7) 16%–18%

    (3) 4%–6%   (8) 19%–21%

    (4) 7%–9%   (9) 22% or more

    (5) 10%–12%

9. _____ Compared to last year at this same time, how would you rate the overall performance of your organizational unit?

    (1) Much Lower

    (2) Lower

    (3) Slightly Lower

    (4) About the Same

    (5) Slightly Higher

    (6) Higher

    (7) Much Higher

10. _____ Compared to your best worldwide competition, how has your unit performed this past year?

    (1) Substantially Worse

    (2) Somewhat Worse

    (3) About the Same

    (4) Somewhat Better

    (5) Substantially Better

Appendix C
Hints for Initiating Organizational
Culture Change in Each Quadrant

The purpose of this appendix is to stimulate your thinking about activities or behaviors that can move the organization toward the desired future culture. It is intended only to provide some starting notions and to stimulate creative thought on your part. Often managers indicate they know where they want to go (for example, "to increase emphasis in the adhocracy quadrant"), but they don't know where to begin—what actions to initiate or what to tackle first. These lists of actions have been derived from the suggestions of numerous managers who have initiated culture change, but because each organization may be different, many of them may not be relevant to your particular circumstances. Therefore, in considering what you want to accomplish in each quadrant, select the ideas most relevant to your circumstances. To these suggestions, add others that you generate in a brainstorming session. Choose the ideas from this list that will be most powerful in beginning the process of culture change. Remember not to try too many initiatives at once. Focus your efforts on a few powerful alternatives.

Clan Culture

- Establish a 360-degree evaluation system to assess the leadership practices of all senior managers. That is, get evaluative input from subordinates, peers, and superiors. See that every senior manager, including the CEO, is assisted in analyzing the data, hearing the painful messages, and planning for better performance.

- Design a career development program that emphasizes interunit mobility and will contribute to cross-functional communication.

- Institute an effective employee survey program that will allow for systematically monitoring employee attitudes and ideas. Establish employee teams to work on making changes identified in the survey.

- Involve employees in all phases of strategic planning.

- Develop programs to increase the facilitation and team-building skills of the workforce.

- Identify the longest-standing intergroup conflicts. Analyze those conflicts, and design a systematic set of interventions for transcending them.

- Assess and improve the processes associated with employee diversity.

- Examine the expectation systems that actually drive the behaviors of middle managers. Alter the incentives so that the middle managers behave in more empowered and innovative ways.

- As part of the empowerment process, move more decisions in such areas as pay raises and budgets to lower levels.

- Be sure there is an effective succession plan in place.

- Develop a training program for middle managers that allows them to better understand the strategic pressures on the organization and that conveys how their role must change for the company to be more effective.

- Energize the employee recognition system. Empower managers to use resources to reward extra effort.

- Implement a benefits program that allows each employee to select options. For example, within a set amount, allow the individual to choose the desired level of medical, dental, life, and disability insurance coverage.

- Create an internal university. Create an overall educational function that has a systematic training strategy for educational needs at every level of the unit.

- Make an assessment of the training needs in each unit, prioritize the needs, and develop programs to meet the needs. Have people inside the unit do the training.

- Increase attendance in training programs by requiring the supervisors of all participants who do not attend the program to report in writing the reason for the absence.

- Build cross-functional teamwork by holding a daily fifteen-minute meeting of all managers. The agenda is to identify all items requiring coordination between units. Problems are solved outside the meeting.

- Build cross-functional teamwork by establishing an operational planning group that provides a plan of the day and a three-day view into the future.

- Senior management holds a monthly "skip level" meeting with different cross-sectional groups of lower-level employees to identify problems and surface suggestions for better cross-functional coordination.

- Constantly monitor the problems of first-line supervisors, and see that they are cared for. Be sure that they are paid better than their subordinates.

- Empower first-line supervisors by eliminating the layer of supervision directly above them. Chart all responsibilities that need to be performed, provide the necessary training, and totally empower the first-line supervisors to make key decisions and react quickly to the needs at hand.

- Revolutionize the performance evaluation system by making subordinates' assessments of a superior's performance a part of evaluations of supervisory and management personnel.

- Improve the relationships between support and line operations. Use a facilitator to help each support group identify its strengths and weaknesses in providing support. Help the line groups identify their key support needs. Hold sessions for the groups to explore their relationship and develop a new set of expectations for working together.

- Increase the effectiveness of the employee suggestion system. Benchmark the best system in other organizations, and upgrade your current system.

Adhocracy Culture

- Analyze the organization's key values in terms of emphasis on adhocracy values. Encourage more focus on managing the future.

- Make a critical analysis of the current vision statement. Does it provide both cognitive and emotional direction? Does it inspire creative initiative?

- Employ a planning process that operates on a five-year time horizon and involves both short- and long-term planning. See that the planning process stretches current assumptions.

- Move from a hierarchical to a flexible structure that emphasizes speed and agility.

- Identify the major emerging issues of concern in the company, and apply the "one voice" concept by making one champion responsible for each emerging issue.

- Forecast customer demand at all points of contact, and find ways to exceed those demands.

- Ask a task force of first-line people to conceptualize new strategies for expanding markets and developing new businesses.

- Read extensively on the concept of continuous improvement. Find out what is being done successfully in other places.

- Hold a meeting to review the differences between transformational and transitional leadership, and explore the implications of the two concepts for making change in your unit.

- Bring all disciplines and departments into the first stages of the design process for new services and products. Be sure that the customer is represented.

- Develop systems to encourage, measure, and reward innovative behavior at all levels of the system.

- Make a hard assessment of the overall behavior of the corporation as a citizen of the community. What problems does it cause? What contributions does it make? Review the possibilities for change. Get outside perspectives on these issues.

- Develop a reading program on the topic of creating and implementing change.

- Explore the possibility of organizing around externally driven tasks rather than current internal functions. Read up on process improvement and organizational reengineering.

- Assign someone to read the literature on the concept of organizational learning. Determine if your unit is an effective learning organization. Make changes to improve the capacity of your organization to learn more effectively.

- Put all employees through a training program that includes the practical applications of creative thinking, the strategic reasons for increased responsiveness, and the basic principles of organizational innovation.

- Have the CEO hold focus group interviews with middle managers to determine how well they understand the direction of the company. Gather their recommendations on how to make the direction more clear.

- Explore the use of new technology, especially information technology, to create new alternatives faster based on a wider variety of information sources.

- Make a conscious effort to move from an orientation of giving customers what they need to giving customers what they would like, to surprising and delighting customers with products and services that solve problems that they don't expect to be solved.

- Keep track of the amount of time leaders in your organization spend on positioning the organization for the future, as opposed to coping with the present.

- Hold celebrations and internal organization "trade shows" that allow employees to show off their new, underdeveloped, experimental ideas. Celebrate trial-and-error learning.

- Develop visible rewards that recognize the creativity and innovation of employees, teams, and units. Recognize not only good ideas but also orchestrating and sponsoring activities that help new ideas get developed and adopted.

Market Culture

- Review the vision, values, goals, objectives, and measures being used at the corporate level. Develop your own version for your unit. Implement them the way you think the CEO should have implemented them at the corporate level.

- Reexamine or reinvent the processes associated with customer contacts and the flow of information from the customer through the organization.

- Consider the needs of special segments of the customer population. Find new ways to respond to them. For example, try aligning billing practices with the late-month income patterns of senior citizens.

- Examine your current time-to-market response time, and make comparisons with key competitors. Identify ways to be more competitive on response time.

- Constantly analyze the evolution of the market by holding exploratory focus group sessions with the people most closely associated with the market.

- Study the best-quality achievements of competitors, and share them with employees. Ask for suggestions on how to be more competitive.

- Establish a performance improvement program in which every employee is asked to suggest items that lead directly to increased profitability, productivity, quality, or responsiveness.

- Hold meetings to acquaint investors with your strategic plans and to meet your key management personnel.

- Assess the need for a more global perspective among the members of your unit, and provide opportunities to broaden and globalize their perspectives.

- Develop a rationalized corporate contributions program. Track the external organizations that approach your organization for contributions and support. Provide support to the external organizations that fit your strategic values system and that create mutually advantageous partnerships.

- Employ an outside marketing firm to survey customer satisfaction. Assess the levels of courtesy, competence, and concern that are shown by your employees.

- Implement the concept of customer alliances. Develop programs of partnership with your largest customers. Provide opportunities for their input into your decision-making processes just as a partner would participate in a joint financial deal.

- Hold a retreat with all managers. Combine hard-nosed reviews and improvement proposals with measurement and accountability sessions.

- Hold focus group interviews with customers to obtain their current expectations and levels of satisfaction with services and products.

- Increase the sense of integrity that customers see in your organization. Develop a customer education system to help customers make informed choices in services and products of the type you provide.

- Analyze your organization's competencies, and assess them against anticipated future demands. Develop a program of competency acquisition.

- Develop an assessment that evaluates the contributions to overall corporate competitiveness made by every unit. Based on the evaluations, establish systems whereby every unit can become a better contributor to overall competitiveness.

- Create a system whereby all customer requests and questions can be satisfied with just one telephone call at a single point of contact.

- Evaluate the contribution of your unit to the strategic partnering efforts of the company.

- Use competitive benchmarking in your change efforts. Keep your people aware of the best practices going on elsewhere.

- Reinforce the concept of the profit center. Emphasize the profit responsibility of every unit, including staff units.

- Increase the standards used in evaluating performance. Aggressively remove all poor performers. Put poor performance units on notice.

- Form a team to assess the growth potential of core businesses and identify potential new high-growth areas.

- Apply for the Baldrige Award or ISO 9000, or engage in a similar action that will hold the internal processes responsible to some form of outside assessment and evaluation. This will force the entire organization to stretch.

- Implement a total quality management system.

- Conduct a study to determine how best to limit future retiree liabilities.

- Assign someone to read the current literature on competitor intelligence. Have that person assess the state of the unit's mechanisms of competitive intelligence and recommend appropriate changes.

- Identify "sharp-pointed prods," outrageous goals and targets that require performance levels never before obtained.

Hierarchy Culture

- Examine the time it takes between customer requests for services and products and actual delivery. Redesign systems that will cut the time in half.

- Hold an annual audit to determine if all measurement and accounting systems are focused on the desired future organization rather than on present practice.

- Develop evaluation systems wherein customer feedback can have an immediate impact on organizational practices.

- Reduce costs by 5 percent every year for the next five years.

- Evaluate every practice and process in each unit. Establish measurement criteria and methods for maintaining accountability.

- Consider using technology that will reduce paperwork and move the unit toward the concept of paperless organization.

- Consider the concept of "rightsizing" the organization. Don't just look to reduce the number of people in the organization; be prepared to increase the number of people where needed.

- Establish a "work-out" program. Although the size of the workforce may be reduced, the amount of work often stays the same or even increases. Take work out of the system.

- Increase the capacity for information to flow through the system, particularly in times of high tension or crisis.

- Select the operational tasks that are most basic and widespread, and consider technological possibilities for reducing costs through a decentralizing process.

- Examine possibilities for establishing more efficient inventory control by instituting "just in time" practices.

- Institute a health and safety audit. Develop a system to assess and improve health and safety, and hold an annual audit that closely examines all practices.

- Put a project manager in charge of building a common system that will allow all departments to access all information from anywhere in the system.

- Reduce cycle time by moving centralized functions that can be performed by individual units to the individual units. Consider, for example, desktop publishing.

- Improve the preventive maintenance program.

- If high-level managers spend significant amounts of time approving expenditures they know little about or for low dollar amounts, modify the process so that lower-level people have final sign-off.

- Use process improvement audits. Compare the results to industry standards. Analyze the best practices used elsewhere.

- Do an assessment of the disruptions that affect your organization. Develop plans for crisis prevention and crisis response.

- Do an analysis of the physical location of all units, and compare it with an analysis of internal customer relationships. Review what changes might be possible to facilitate better coordination among internal customers.

- Develop a real-time audit team to work on each of the biggest projects in the organization. These teams will audit decisions while they are being made rather than long afterward.

- Determine the yearly operating cost for all information systems, and determine if each dollar is being spent appropriately.

- Place a one-year freeze on the purchase of new computers. Spend this time discovering how to allocate the dollars for computers more effectively.

- Assess the degree to which the budgeting process is linked with the resource planning process, and make appropriate changes.

- Contract with a single maintenance provider, at a reduced cost, to serve all computer maintenance needs in the organization.

- Review the impacts of every corporate policy and procedure now in place. Recommend appropriate reductions.

- Institute an internal communications program that more effectively informs people of events, activities, and programs. Use the latest technology for such a system.

- Remove all senior managers, no matter how successful, whose behavior does not reflect the values espoused by the company.

- Do a complete inventory of the company's equipment assets every five years. Each time this is done, improve the process by implementing the latest technological breakthroughs.

- Decentralize authority from central corporate bodies so that each unit or plant director has control of all budgets within the unit.

Appendix D
Suggestions for Improving
Personal Management
Competencies

The following suggestions may be useful if you desire to improve your management competency in the primary skill areas identified for each quadrant in Figure 6.1. The list is designed to be a thought starter or a supplement to the items on the management skills survey itself. These lists are not intended to be comprehensive. Only one or two of the suggestions on the list may be relevant to your job, but they may stimulate you to think of other ideas. As you form your personal improvement plan, find ways to implement these suggestions in your managerial role.

Clan Quadrant

Managing Teams

- Establish a clear, overarching goal or vision for the team. Clearly identify what the team's mission is.
- Establish specific targets and objectives, with deadlines, that the team can accomplish.
- Hold a retreat or an extended meeting to launch the team's activities, to explain the mission, to clarify roles and expectations, and to build cohesion among team members.
- Schedule a time for regular team meetings.
- Diagnose the team's stage of development. In different stages, different leadership roles are most effective (for example, more direction is needed in early stages, more delegation in later stages).

- The ideal team size is five to nine people, depending on the complexity of the task and the information needed. Try to keep team membership stable and within these limits.

- Keep everyone on the team informed of all relevant information.

- Assure a free flow of communication and an exchange of ideas by sponsoring team members who don't participate willingly, keeping any single person or point of view from dominating the team meetings, and asking pointed questions of team members. Seek input from every single team member.

- Clarify the roles that each team member should play. Pay attention to task roles, process monitoring roles, integrator roles, and so on.

- Identify the resources each team member brings to the group, and help make those resources available to all team members.

- In cross-functional teams, keep each member's "back home" unit informed on the progress being made by the team. This helps the team member's political credibility, fosters buy-in, and eliminates last-minute surprises.

- Sponsor informal events that help build team cohesiveness (such as getting together after hours, including spouses or part- ners in a meeting, or celebrating a team member's birthday).

- Be accessible to team members to answer questions, pass along information, show interest and involvement, and model appro- priate behaviors.

- Be a good listener in team meetings. If you are leading the team, avoid stating your opinions and perspectives up front. Seek input from others before stating conclusions or your per- spective. Restate the comments of others to make sure you un- derstand, especially if they disagree with your point of view.

- In team meetings, continually remind members of team ob- jectives, agreements reached up to now, and what's left to accomplish.

- When team members disagree or the team experiences conflict, don't take sides. Avoid making it personal, keep it issues-centered, label it and deal with it directly, and help the team seek alternative solutions.

- Seek feedback from team members about what you do that facilitates effective team meetings and what you do that inhibits effective team meetings.

- Stand up for your team members, especially when they are not present. Compliment them in public. Correct them only in private.

Managing Interpersonal Relationships

- Hold a meeting with your associates to review the meaning of the feedback you received from this questionnaire.

- At least once each day, praise and express appreciation for those with whom you work.

- Communicate a feeling of personal caring for those you manage by telling them you appreciate their efforts, sending them a note, or telling their spouse or family member how valuable they are to the organization. Remember birthdays, holidays, and special occasions.

- Be clear about your expectations for coworkers' performance. That way, they won't be frustrated by uncertainty and you won't be disappointed in having them not do as you'd like. Try to reduce ambiguity in your relationships.

- Be congruent and consistent in your interpersonal interactions by making sure that your behavior and words match your feelings and thoughts. Avoid hidden agendas and phoniness.

- Increase your accessibility to those with whom you work. You need not be accessible all the time, but there should be some time when they can get to you with their concerns, problems, or successes.

- Ask those with whom you work two questions: (1) What do I do that bothers you the most or that creates obstacles for your being more successful? (2) What can I do to improve our relationship? Be prepared to listen carefully, to ask questions to fully understand what is being said, and to work toward a mutually satisfactory change.

- In interactions with others, ask them questions about themselves and their interests. Talk more about them than you do about you. Find out about something they've done that they feel good about.

- Practice "management by walking around" in your work. Visit the turf of subordinates.

- Instead of avoiding people with whom you have a conflict or bad feelings, approach them directly. Hold a discussion with them, first about neutral, objective topics and then about the problem you have experienced between you.

- Put yourself in the shoes of a coworker. Imagine what the person would expect of you. What would your colleague like you to change?

- Listen carefully to others as they speak to you. Maintain eye contact. When there is a chance that you may have misunderstood something, repeat or restate what you think you heard.

- Use multiple response types when discussing concerns or problems with others: reflecting, probing, pacifying, interpretive, directive, and so on. Seek information and show understanding before you give advice or express an opinion.

- In problem situations or disagreements, make communication supportive by relying more on descriptive communication than on evaluative communication. In other words, describe the objective, what happened, what your reaction is or what the consequences are, and what solution you suggest.

- Empower those with whom you work by helping them increase their personal competence, choices, security, and trust in the work setting.

- Differentiate between coaching and counseling situations. In coaching situations, advice, direction, or information is needed because of a problem with ability or understanding. In counseling situations, support, understanding, or motivation is needed because of a problem with attitude, personality, or emotions.

Managing the Development of Others

- Make time available to observe, evaluate, and coach the performance of your subordinates. Be clear about the level of performance they expect of themselves, as well as the level expected by the organization. Help them exceed expectations.

- Establish SMART goals with your subordinates—*specific, measurable, aligned* to the organization's mission, *reachable* but still a stretch, and *time-bound*. Identify specific actions they can take to accomplish the goals—a regular system of reporting and accountability and a reward for accomplishing the goals.

- When assigning work to others, follow principles of effective delegation by (1) delegating clearly and completely, (2) allowing participation in deciding what is delegated, (3) matching authority with responsibility, (4) working within the established structure, (5) providing adequate support, (6) maintaining accountability for results, (7) delegating consistently, and (8) avoiding upward delegation.

- Model the kind of behavior you wish to foster in others. Set the example, and help others know how to improve through demonstration.

- Celebrate the successes of those with whom you work. Look for praiseworthy incidents, accomplishments, or attributes. Celebrate publicly.

- Find ways to get other people up front. Provide chances for them to make presentations, to conduct meetings, to take assignments that will provide them some visibility.

- Ensure that the work of your subordinates has these five characteristics: (1) task variety, (2) task identity, (3) task significance, (4) autonomy, and (5) feedback.

- Ensure that subordinates are empowered. That is, help them develop a sense of self-efficacy, self-determination, personal control, meaningfulness, and trust.

- Encourage and support your people in taking risks. Avoid punishing people when they try something new and fail. Cultivate a sense of excitement with trying something that might produce an improvement, but make certain that learning occurs from mistakes. Ensure that those who fail identify clearly what lessons were learned.

- Give subordinates regular feedback about their work performance and your feelings about them. Because only the recipient can judge how much feedback is enough, ask subordinates periodically if they get enough feedback from you.

- Provide opportunities for your people to learn new tasks. Enrich and expand their jobs by adding responsibilities that require the learning of new skills and abilities.

- Turn students into teachers. Ensure that your subordinates not only learn new things but also have a chance to teach those things to others. Learning is more fun and more effective when what is learned is passed on to others. Make certain that subordinates have a chance to teach. Reward expanded knowledge, skill, and information dissemination.

- Give subordinates a chance to learn your job. Help them learn the responsibilities associated with one level above their current organization position.

- Make a list of strengths and weaknesses of each of your people. Identify experiences or training that will help address those weaknesses. Share your recommendations for development, and help them reach their goals.

- Provide opportunities for subordinates to evaluate you and one another. Have them identify the standards that are most important, the levels of performance they observe, and suggestions for improvement. Maturity and insight are facilitated if people are required to specify exact standards and to assess how well they are achieved.

- Make it a priority to help others become better performers than they are now.

Adhocracy Quadrant

Managing Innovation

- Institute a token penalty system for use when people in your organization use "creativity killers" such as "We already tried that," "It'll never work," "It's against policy," or "The boss won't like it."

- Establish goals, and hold people accountable for producing innovative ideas. Make that a part of everyone's job description.

- Read broadly in fields not directly related to your area of expertise. Talk to people about their ideas and what they're thinking about, not just about results and outcomes. Start a conversation with "What have you learned lately?" Actively seek out new ideas, new thoughts, and new perspectives. Keep a notebook or note cards to record the interesting ideas you hear.

- Hold idea-sharing or idea-blending events in your work setting, such as internal trade shows, cross-functional task forces, symposia, book reviews, or focus groups. The idea is to address questions such as "What's new?" "What have you been thinking about?" and "What problem do you have that you don't expect anyone to solve?"

- Establish a practice field, separated from normal daily work, where new ideas can be tried out and low-cost experimentation can occur. This might include an actual physical location, time off, or extra resources.

- Form teams and task forces where a formal minority report is expected to be filed, where at least one person is assigned the task of finding alternative viewpoints or exceptions to the group's recommendations, or where other mechanisms are used to create divergence.

- Monitor regularly and closely the expectations, complaints, and preferences of customers. Reject nothing out of hand as outrageous or impossible. Use their ideas to stimulate different ways to approach work. Borrow ideas shamelessly.

- Reward not only idea champions and those who generate new approaches to work but also sponsors or mentors of those ideas or approaches, as well as orchestrators or facilitators who help the ideas get disseminated and implemented more widely. Successful innovation takes all three roles: idea champions, sponsors, and orchestrators.

- Encourage action learning among your people. Try things first, and then analyze what you have learned from your success or failure. Don't wait until you are certain of success before you take action.

- The best hitters in baseball succeed about 33 percent of the time. Consider whether you can expect anything more from your people if you are really expecting innovation. Create a climate where people feel free to fail and to admit it.

- Ask for feedback from those with whom you work regarding what inhibits them from generating new ideas.

- Make success visible. Celebrate even small wins. Provide a way for people involved in successful new processes or products to reap rewards from their innovations.

- Encourage and reward not only big changes and visible innovations but also small, incremental, continuous improvements. Look for trends indicating minor but never-ending improvements in addition to major improvements.

- Focus more on how work is accomplished than on what is accomplished in terms of new approaches. Construct process flowcharts and identify redundancies, irrelevancies, and work that adds no value. Encourage change in the *how* first, and the *what* will naturally follow.

- When considering a difficult problem, ask *why* at least five times in a row. This forces a search for root causes of problems, generates new ideas for approaching the problem, and gets away from treating symptoms instead of the core problem.

- Try out ideas first on a pilot basis. Don't revolutionize the entire organization until you have experimented first on a small-scale basis.

Managing the Future

- Hold an off-site meeting with your direct subordinates to articulate a vision, clarify its wording and key principles, and generate major strategies for accomplishing it. Get participation and buy-in from all key players.

- Make a list of obstacles that impede what you hope to achieve in the future. What stands in the way of your outstanding success? Now reconsider each item on the list, interpreting each obstacle as a surmountable challenge. How can the impediment be made into an opportunity?

- Keep track of trends and predictions for the future of your industry or sector. Monitor what is happening with your competitors not just domestically but around the world. Spend some time each month thinking ten years ahead. Don't get stuck in automatic short-term thinking.

- Identify some cutting-edge organizations that tend to establish trends in one business or sector. They need not be in your industry or sector. Based on what you observe, project a future for your organization. What would you have to be like to be considered world-class?

- Get participation by others in the formulation of your organization's vision and in the strategies to accomplish that vision. Formulating a vision for your organization should not be a one-person activity. Get feedback on your vision statement, and get ideas about how best to accomplish it.

- Write a personal vision statement. Articulate clearly what you feel passionately about and what legacy you'd like to leave as a manager. Where do you want to be in five years? (This is different from your organization's vision statement.)

- Live your life so as to exemplify the principles of your vision. Exemplify what you have articulated. Walk the talk. Don't be hypocritical. Be an example of what you want others to be.

- What stories or incidents in your own organization exemplify progress toward your vision of the future? Disseminate these motivational stories, and repeat them often. Help make them part of the folklore that defines success in your organization.

- Communicate your vision of the future often, consistently, and in a variety of ways. Never give a public presentation without communicating your vision in some way. Express it out loud, in written form, and by your behavior.

- Provide opportunities for subordinates to become teachers of the vision. Structure opportunities where others can articulate and explain your vision. Hold them accountable for disseminating the vision to their subordinates.

- In articulating a vision, make sure to honor the past. Don't denigrate or throw away the strengths and successes of the past while creating a new future. On the other hand, make certain that your vision is seen as a step forward and a new direction, not more of the same.

- Ask each of your subordinates and each unit within your organization to generate its own vision statement. Each vision statement should be consistent with the basic principles and values of the overall organizational vision. However, unit and personal vision statements should identify the unique attributes and mission of each unit and person.

- Make certain that the organization's vision statement contains simple, straightforward language; that it is short enough to be memorized; and that it is expressed using superlatives and passionate language. The language of the vision should capture the hearts as well as the minds of your people. It should be memorable but not cutesy or slogan-centered.

- Invite people to challenge the vision and to modify it at the margins but then to commit to it. Empower people to use the vision as their guide while taking independent action based on it.

- Provide opportunities for people to commit to the vision publicly. The more public the commitment, the more likely the commitment will stick. Provide opportunities for your subordinates to orient someone else about the vision, to explain it in a presentation, or to defend one of its principles in front of others.

Managing Continuous Improvement

- Measure improvement, not just task or goal accomplishment.
- Establish a reward system that recognizes and celebrates improvement, not just doing the job right.
- Specify in all job descriptions the expectation that generating ideas for improvement is a never-ending responsibility. Not only are people expected to do the job perfectly, but they are also expected to improve it.
- Establish a suggestion system in which feedback is provided within twenty-four hours. Even if no progress has been made evaluating or implementing a suggestion, give feedback to that effect anyway to the person who offered it.
- Legitimize and acknowledge improvements that save as little as one second or one cent. Communicate the fact that no improvement is too small to be important.
- Make continuous improvement a key feature of the vision you articulate for your own unit.
- Set aside some time, for yourself and for your subordinates, to think, analyze, and ponder. Get off the fast track of activity

regularly so that ideas can be generated for improvements to the status quo.

- Give work on process improvements higher priority than work on product or outcome improvements.

- Make certain that everyone is his or her own monitor or checker. All mistakes should be corrected by the person who made them. Ensure that people get feedback about and learn from their mistakes.

- Reward and recognize improvement trends as well as big ideas. Make sure that people are compensated for small wins. Post results.

- Make it easy for employees, as well as customers, to complain and to give suggestions. Make the assumption that more input is better, and actively seek out improvement ideas from employees and customers.

- Give customers what they want the first time, every time; then work toward exceeding those expectations. Surprise and delight them with levels of service they would never have expected or requested.

- Institute regular audits of each unit in your organization to find ways to improve it. Use cross-functional teams, even outsiders, so that fresh perspectives help generate new ideas.

- Establish past performance as the standard against which you measure success. Even if you are the best in the business, replace that external standard with the internal standard of improvement.

- Constantly thank people for the work they do, for their ideas, for their improvements, and for their efforts.

- Never let twenty-four hours go by without asking some customers what they want. Constant asking will produce a constant flow of ideas.

- Model continuous improvement in your own life. Identify ways in your personal life, as well as in your work, that you can continuously improve. Walk the talk.

Market Quadrant

Managing Competitiveness

- Keep track of how your best competitors are performing. Read trade journals, business publications, and news clippings. Consider hiring researchers to gather data on an ongoing basis on the performance and strategies of firms in your industry or sector.

- Benchmark the best practices in the best organizations throughout the world. What are they doing differently from you? What are they planning to do in the future? What key success factors account for their achievements?

- Find ways to learn from successes by other units inside your organization. Hold discussion groups, take people to lunch, and read the internal organization publications of other units to highlight your own strengths and weaknesses and to pick up new ideas.

- Identify your unit's core competencies and strategic advantages. What is it that makes your organization unique? What competencies serve as the life blood of your organization—that are shared by all key employees, are typified by your strategy, and account for your competitive success?

- Conduct a formal SWOT analysis, listing *strengths*, *weaknesses*, *opportunities*, and *threats*. Involve your subordinates as well as your key customers.

- Don't tolerate anything but world-class quality in your products and services. Communicate the message that if it isn't your best effort, your best thinking, or your best idea, it is unacceptable.

- Establish clear priorities. Not everything you can do adds value. Make your most important priorities the things that add value to the ultimate customer.

- Improve the speed and timeliness of your outputs. Identify where the bottlenecks are, where the extra sign-offs are, where the redundancies are, and where the drags are in the system. Eliminate, redesign, or change the things that slow you down.

- Draw flowcharts of all the key processes in your organization. Get everyone involved in the flowcharts. Assign everyone the task of both reducing the number of steps and increasing the speed of the processes that are used by at least 20 percent.

- Make certain that every person in your organization can name his or her three most crucial customers.

- Identify the amount of time it takes to (1) develop a new product, (2) make an important decision, (3) produce one unit of output, (4) respond to a customer complaint, (5) learn the root cause of a mistake. Cut the time in half.

- Give customers what they want the first time, every time; then work toward exceeding those expectations. Surprise and delight them with levels of service they would never have expected or requested.

- Prevent errors from occurring, rather than finding and fixing mistakes already made. Make certain that all employees understand and use, to the extent appropriate, the seven statistical management tools for achieving quality (SPC, Pareto charts, design of experiments).

- Collect data on an ongoing basis about adverse indicators of performance such as complaints, recalls, refunds, warranty costs, replacements, repeat service, returns, grievances, worker complaints, and absenteeism. Work daily to reduce these adverse indicators.

- Don't collect too much data. Don't require reports that are not used. Make certain that the information gathered in reports is used for improvement. Regularly give feedback to those who provide the data.

- Make a continuous effort to downsize the organization. That doesn't mean reducing headcount. It means finding ways to reduce resource requirements and costs while increasing efficiency.

- Celebrate success. Vince Lombardi is said to have asked, "If winning isn't important, why do they keep score?" Instill an attitude of winning in your people by enthusiastically celebrating victories, even small ones.

- Do business with your competitors once in a while. Identify what they do better than you.

Energizing Employees

- Determine what rewards and incentives are most desired by people in your unit. Establish an incentive system that includes frequently administered nonmonetary rewards.

- Minimize the time lag between your people's performance and the feedback they receive. Immediate recognition is far more effective than a delayed reward.

- Recognize and celebrate small wins.

- Administer discipline consistently and fairly, but always use it as a training and development experience. Discipline on the basis of work performance compared to a standard. Never discipline on the basis of personal attributes or noncontrollable attributes (such as age or gender), and never discipline in public. Make certain that lessons to be learned are given more emphasis than things done wrong.

- Encourage aggressiveness and achievement among your people where they push each other to be more productive. Try internal competitions or limited-time contests. Make certain that these are always focused on the organization's goal, that they are not personalized, and that they are equitably administered.

- Establish mentors in your organization who can help increase the effort and performance level of new people. Mentors should constantly push for better performance.

- Establish SMART goals with your subordinates—*specific, measurable, aligned* to the organization's mission, *reachable* but still a stretch, and *time-bound*. Identify the specific action steps required to reach each goal, the report steps to be used to maintain accountability, the indicators of success, the time frame in which the goals will be accomplished, and the expected benefits and rewards of successful goal achievement.

- Maintain a positive attitude around your employees and those who look to you for direction. The positive energy in the organization is highly dependent on the personal mood and behavior of the leader.

- Act as a cheerleader for those you manage. Sponsor them to outsiders, facilitate their success, recognize their accomplishments, and treat them like family.

- Reduce all ambiguity about where you want the organization to go and why. Be specific and firm in articulating your vision.

- Ask your subordinates regularly such questions as "How is your work going?" "What do you enjoy the most and the least?" "How can I help you succeed?" and "What could be improved in our organization?"

- Manage by walking around. Be visible and accessible to your people.

- Make certain that the work assigned to subordinates has (1) skill variety, (2) task identity—responsibility for a complete or whole task, (3) task significance, (4) autonomy, and (5) feedback on results.

- Enhance the power of your people by assisting them in (1) gaining more access to important information that they need, (2) increasing their flexibility and discretion in their work, (3) becoming more visible in the organization, and (4) seeing more clearly the relevance of their outputs.

- Express confidence in the abilities of your subordinates. When ability problems exist, provide coaching.

Managing Customer Service

- Establish a procedure for assessing the needs and expectations of your customers, both inside and outside your unit. Collect those data on an ongoing basis, not just once. Because expectations continue to rise, monitor changes and trends.

- After you deliver your product or service, continuously monitor how well you met the needs and expectations of your customers.

- Provide opportunities at some point for every employee to interact face-to-face with your external customers.

- Eliminate activities that don't have a payoff for customers. If an action doesn't improve service, add value to the product, or create customer loyalty, don't do it.

- Clarify who your most important internal and external customers are. Ensure that no employee is unclear about who his or her most important customers are.

- Include customer service as a key criterion in the performance appraisal of all employees. Appraise and reward customer service performance for every employee.

- Make it easy for customers to complain. Seek out complaints. The more you know, the better the service you can provide and the more likely you are to meet or exceed expectations.

- Don't go twenty-four hours without asking some customers in your organization how you're doing, what they like and don't like, whether you are meeting their expectations, and so on.

- Always discover the reasons why your customers are satisfied or dissatisfied. Don't be satisfied with just knowing the level of customer satisfaction. Know why it is at that level.

- When a mistake is made, go the extra mile to make things right. Include something extra every time.

- Give everyone who deals with the ultimate customer the authority to resolve concerns on the spot. Eliminate sign-offs with higher-ups unless they relate to gathering information or obtaining resources not under the control of the customer contact employee. Train employees to make decisions in favor of the customer while not bankrupting the organization.

- "Shop" from competitors once in a while to see what you can learn. Also "shop" from your own organization to see what you can learn. Highlight areas needing improvement that relate to the customer interface.

- Train customers to know what to expect when they do business with you. Be clear about what you do and don't provide. Tell them how you do business. Then recognize good customers. Thank them. Give them something extra.

- Be willing to be taken advantage of occasionally by a customer. Even when customers are wrong, if you give them what they want, you generate customer loyalty and send a loud message throughout the organization. Since 99 percent of the people are honest, don't waste time protecting yourself against the 1 percent who aren't.

- When providing "extra-mile" customer service, if you wouldn't charge a friend for the service, don't charge your customer.

- Gather information from potential customers and, especially, from former customers. Before you have a chance to serve people, learn their preferences and expectations. After a customer has chosen to be served by someone else, ask why. Listen.

- Reward your most frequent customers.

- Celebrate your best customer service providers. Make customer service a key part of your employee appraisal system. (That means that subordinates may evaluate their bosses.)

- Treat internal customers (employees) the same as you treat external (ultimate) customers—extremely well.

Hierarchy Quadrant

Managing Acculturation

- Meet personally with each of the employees that you manage when they first join your unit, in order to clarify expectations and answer questions.

- Make certain that all employees have a formal orientation session on the traditions, values, vision, and strategies of your organization. Include senior executives, as well as peers, in the orientation session.

- Formulate and print out a standard set of procedures and policies that helps everyone know how to get work done in your unit. Make certain that everyone has a copy.

- Provide opportunities to employees for job rotation. Help them learn to do more jobs than just their primary one. Provide opportunities for them to get outside the area of their specialty.

- Help employees get exposed to a variety of organizational perspectives by involving them in cross-functional and cross-level teams.

- Make certain your subordinates have all the information they need to succeed. Keep them informed of what is going on in the organization. Pass along relevant information even if they don't request it (such as journal articles, memos, newspaper clippings, or certain measures of performance).

- Provide regular, ongoing feedback to subordinates on their work performance, their strengths, and their weaknesses.

- Help reduce the ambiguity and complexity of information for your subordinates. Clarify or interpret confusing data.

- Schedule informative socialization activities for individuals in your unit. Involve family members or partners. Find ways to interact outside the formal roles associated with the organization.

- Make certain that all employees know why they are doing what they're doing, how it fits into the broader picture, and what ultimate impact it has on customers.

- Help employees construct process maps of their roles and responsibilities. Make certain that they know how they fit into the organization. Assist them in identifying blank spots and overlaps in their responsibilities.

- Involve others in formulating an organizational vision statement. Involve them in devising strategies to accomplish that vision. Seek feedback from them on the meaning of the vision statement, and get their ideas about how to best accomplish it.

- Have all subordinates write a personal vision statement. Have them articulate clearly what they feel passionately about and what legacy they'd like to leave the organization. Where do they want to be in five years?

- Create a mentoring system for inexperienced people or new employees. Assignments can be formal or informal. The role of mentors is to help ensure acculturation, to monitor and facilitate improvement, and to help remove obstacles to success.

Managing the Control System

- Establish a monitoring system that allows you to know how your unit is performing daily on critical performance indicators.

- Establish a budget for all critical resources (money, time, task assignments, expertise, and so on). Identify ways in which each of those critical resources is allocated and expended.

- Analyze the key reports that are produced by and for your unit with a critical eye to ensure their accuracy and usefulness.

- Use a rational, stepwise system for defining, analyzing, and solving problems in your unit. For example, (1) define the problem completely, (2) identify root causes of the problem, (3) generate alternative solutions, (4) analyze the merits of each solution, (5) select the optimal solution, and (6) implement the solution. Publish the procedure (whichever one you choose), and ensure that it is followed throughout the organization.

- Clarify the specific goals and objectives that are to be accomplished by your organization. Identify the specific measures that will determine success.

- Ask tough questions of those who are accountable for performance. Ask *why* at least five times when determining the reasons for specific recommendations. Determine the basic assumptions being made. What information would you need to be certain that the recommendations are right? Ask for it.

- Keep a personal journal and an organizational history. Record significant events, insights, lessons learned, improvements and successes accomplished, and critical indicators of performance.

- Draw flowcharts of all the key processes in your organization. Assemble everyone involved in those processes to analyze overlaps, non-value-added work, obstacles to success, and needed improvements.

- Make sure you have a record of all the talents, resources, and expertise available in your unit. Determine the strengths and weaknesses of each of your employees.

- Have a lifetime for every assignment in the organization. Generate a tickler file to determine when reminders should be made, when results are due, when interim progress reports are due, and so on.

- Have a "to do" list for each day. Complete and sign off on at least one major undertaking every day.

- Separate urgent from important tasks. Prioritize them so that the urgent and important get attention first, the important but not urgent second, and the urgent but not important third.

- Determine the 20 percent of the tasks that produce 80 percent of the results (Pareto's law). Determine specific measures of success for the tasks. Give them the highest priority. Allocate the best talent to them.

- Keep track of time use in your organization and for yourself. How do you spend your time each day? How does the time get used in your organization each day? Determine what needs to be tightened up.

- Hold all short meetings standing up, to ensure that they will remain brief. Establish a time limit, and articulate the agenda before every meeting, even informal meetings. Keep minutes and follow-up on all decision-making meetings. Don't overschedule the day; you want to allow some time for personal thought.

- Insist that subordinates generate solutions to problems, rather than just bringing them to light. Avoid upward delegation.
- Specify the amount of personal initiative that you want subordinates to display when receiving delegated assignments: (1) wait to be told what to do, then act; (2) ask which action should be taken, then follow through; (3) recommend a course of action; (4) report after action has been taken; (5) act independently, with no special report needed.

Managing Coordination

- Establish close working relationships with individuals who represent customer and supplier organizations.
- Effectively manage those above you in the hierarchy by channeling information up to key people, by anticipating requests from them and responding in advance, and by maintaining visibility with individuals and units above you in the organization.
- Hold regular meetings with customers and with suppliers. Coordinate schedules, work flow, requirements, and expectations.
- Manage by walking around. Be accessible and visible to your own people and those with whom you need to coordinate cross-functionally.
- Facilitate cross-functional teamwork in your unit by forming task forces. Invite members from other functions to join to facilitate sharing information with peers in other functions, requesting information or presentations in your unit from members of other units, and so on.
- When complex information (technical information, projections, budget data) comes into your unit, interpret it and share it with the people you manage.
- Generate a list of key stakeholders for your unit for all your core activities: suppliers, service providers, customers, politi-

cally potent outsiders, and so on. Ensure that these stakeholders are kept informed, are contacted regularly for input, and
are asked for expectations.

- Identify at least one champion or sponsor for every core activity in your unit. Make sure that this person also serves as the
liaison to other units.

- Make certain that all necessary information is shared with individuals inside the organization as well as outsiders with
whom you interact. To ensure smooth coordination, avoid
blindsiding or surprising other units or people with information you could have provided sooner.

- Clarify what information you need from other individuals or
other units with whom you coordinate.

- Establish regular meeting times to coordinate with others outside your unit. Do it on a regular basis rather than on a crisis
basis.

- Ensure quality in dividing up work among cross-functional or
cross-unit teams. Fairness should apply to amount of work, visibility attached, closeness to the final output, and number of
resources required.

- Monitor how well communication flows upward, downward,
and horizontally in your organization. How much filtering occurs, and by whom is it done? Can unobstructed messages get
delivered and received? Work to make communication channels obstacle-free.

- Generate process maps for each key process in your unit. Pay
special attention to those that exceed the organization's boundaries, that is, that must be coordinated with other units or hierarchical levels. Use those maps to identify areas of overlap,
information flows that are necessary, and individuals to be
involved.

- Use principles of effective delegation and of empowerment.
For example, delegate clearly and completely, establish parity
between authority and responsibility, allow participation in

delegated assignments, work with the established structure, provide support for delegated tasks, focus accountability of results, and delegate consistently.

- Be meticulous about applying principles of effective meeting management. For example, always have an agenda, be clear about the goals of the meeting, start and end on time, require preparation by each participant, provide important information in advance, keep the meeting focused on the objective, and summarize action steps and agreements at the end of the meeting.

Appendix E
Forms for Plotting Profiles

Figure E.1 Form for Plotting the
Organizational Culture Profile

The Clan Culture

A very friendly place to work where people share a lot of themselves. It is like an extended family. The leaders, or head of the organization, are considered to be mentors and, maybe even, parent figures. The organization is held together by loyalty or tradition. Commitment is high. The organization emphasizes the long-term benefit of human resource development and attaches great importance to cohesion and morale. Success is defined in terms of sensitivity to customers and concern for people. The organization places a premium on teamwork, participation, and consensus.

The Adhocracy Culture

A dynamic, entrepreneurial, and creative place to work. People stick their necks out and take risks. The leaders are considered to be innovators and risk takers. The glue that holds the organization together is commitment to experimentation and innovation. The emphasis is on being on the leading edge. The organization's long-term emphasis is on growth and acquiring new resources. Success means gaining unique and new products or services. Being a product or service leader is important. The organization encourages individual initiative and freedom.

The Hierarchy Culture

A very formalized and structured place to work. Procedures govern what people do. The leaders pride themselves on being good coordinators and organizers, who are efficiency-minded. Maintaining a smooth-running organization is most critical. Formal rules and policies hold the organization together. The long-term concern is on stability and performance with efficient, smooth operations. Success is defined in terms of dependable delivery, smooth scheduling, and low cost. The management of employees is concerned with secure employment and predictability.

The Market Culture

A results-oriented organization. The major concern is getting the job done. People are competitive and goal-oriented. The leaders are hard drivers, producers, and competitors. They are tough and demanding. The glue that holds the organization together is an emphasis on winning. Reputation and success are common concerns. The long-term focus is on competitive actions and achievement of measurable goals and targets. Success is defined in terms of market share and penetration. Competitive pricing and market leadership are important. The organizational style is hard-driving competitiveness.

Figure E.1 Form for Plotting the
Organizational Culture Profile, Cont'd.

The Clan Culture

An organization that focuses on internal maintenance with flexibility, concern for people, and sensitivity to customers.

The Adhocracy Culture

An organization that focuses on external positioning with a high degree of flexibility and individuality.

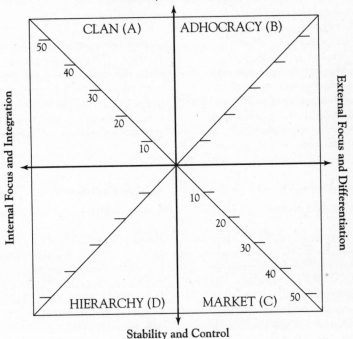

The Hierarchy Culture

An organization that focuses on internal maintenance with a need for stability and control.

The Market Culture

An organization that focuses on external positioning with a need for stability and control.

Figure E.2 Form for Plotting the Management Skills Profile

Clan Culture Leadership Roles

The Facilitator is people- and process-oriented. This person manages conflict and seeks consensus. His or her influence is based on getting people involved in the decision making and problem solving. Participation and openness are actively pursued.

The Mentor is caring and empathic. This person is aware of others and cares for the needs of individuals. His or her influence is based on mutual respect and trust. Morale and commitment are actively pursued.

Adhocracy Culture Leadership Roles

The Innovator is clever and creative. This person envisions change. His or her influence is based on anticipation of a better future and generates hope in others. Innovation and adaptation are actively pursued.

The Visionary is future-oriented in thinking. This person focuses on where the organization is going and emphasizes possibilities as well as probabilities. Strategic direction and continuous improvement of current activities are hallmarks of this style.

Hierarchy Culture Leadership Roles

The Monitor is technically expert and well-informed. This person keeps track of all details and contributes expertise. His or her influence is based on information control. Documentation and information management are actively pursued.

The Coordinator is dependable and reliable. This person maintains the structure and flow of the work. His or her influence is based on situational engineering, managing schedules, giving assignments, physical layout, etc. Stability and control are actively pursued.

Market Culture Leadership Roles

The Competitor is aggressive and decisive. This person actively pursues goals and targets and is energized by competitive situations. Winning is a dominant objective, and the focus is on external competitors and marketplace position.

The Producer is task-oriented and work-focused. This person gets things done through hard work. His or her influence is based on intensity and rational arguments around accomplishing things. Productivity is actively pursued.

Figure E.2 Form for Plotting the Management Skills Profile, Cont'd.

————— Self-ratings

- - - - - Associates' ratings

Figure E.3 Form for Plotting Profiles
for Individual Items on the OCAI

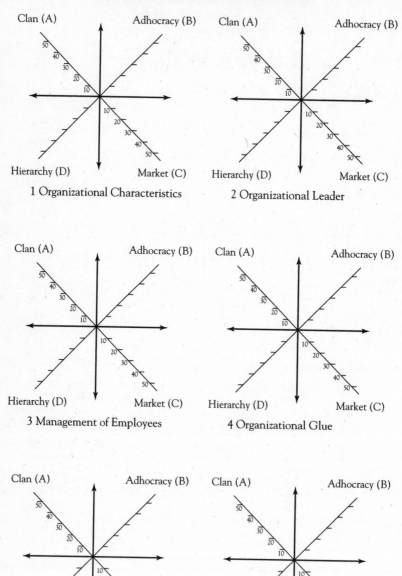

References and
Suggested Reading

Aiken, Michael, and Bacharach, S. B. "Culture and Organizational Structure and Process." In Cornelius Lammers and David J. Hickson (eds.), *Organizations Alike and Unalike*. London: Routledge & Kegan Paul, 1979.

Alpert, Stuart, and Whetten, David A. "Organizational Identity." *Research in Organizational Behavior*, 1985, *7*, 263–502.

Argyris, Chris. *Integrating the Individual and the Organization*. Hoboken, N.J.: Wiley, 1964.

Argyris, Chris. *On Organizational Learning*. Boston: Blackwell, 1993.

Arnold, D. R., and Capella, L. M. "Corporate Culture and the Marketing Concept: A Diagnostic Instrument for Utilities." *Public Utilities Fortnightly*, 1985, *116*, 32–38.

Beyer, Janice, and Cameron, Kim S. *Organizational Culture: Enhancing Organizational Performance*. Washington, D.C.: National Academies Press, 1997.

Blauner, Robert. *Alienation and Freedom*. Chicago: University of Chicago Press, 1964.

Caldwell, Bruce. "Missteps, Miscues." *InformationWeek*, June 20, 1994.

Cameron, Kim S. "The Effectiveness of Ineffectiveness." In *Research in Organizational Behavior*, Vol. 6. Greenwich, Conn.: JAI Press, 1984.

Cameron, Kim S. "Effectiveness as Paradox." *Management Science*, 1986, *32*, 539–553.

Cameron, Kim S. "In What Ways Do Organizations Implement Total Quality?" Paper presented at the annual meeting of the Academy of Management, Las Vegas, Nevada, August 1992.

Cameron, Kim S. "An Empirical Investigation of Quality Culture, Practices, and Outcomes " Paper presented at the annual meeting of the Academy of Management, Dallas, Texas, August 1994.

Cameron, Kim S. "Downsizing, Quality, and Performance." In Robert E. Cole (ed.), *The Fall and Rise of the American Quality Movement*. New York: Oxford University Press, 1995.

Cameron, Kim S. "Techniques for Making Organizations Effective: Some Popular Approaches." In Daniel Druckman, Jerome E. Singer, and Harold

Van Cott (eds.), *Enhancing Organizational Performance*. Washington, D.C.: National Academies Press, 1997.

Cameron, Kim S. "Strategic Organizational Downsizing: An Extreme Case." *Research in Organizational Behavior*, 1998, *20*, 185–229.

Cameron, Kim S. "Ethics, Virtuousness, and Constant Change." In Noel M. Tichy and Andrew R. McGill (eds.), *The Ethical Challenge*. San Francisco: Jossey-Bass, 2003.

Cameron, Kim S. "Good or Not Bad: Standards and Ethics in Managing Change." *Academy of Management Learning and Education Journal*, 2006, *4*.

Cameron, Kim S., Bright, David, and Caza, Arran. "Exploring the Relationships Between Organizational Virtuousness and Performance." *American Behavioral Scientist*, 2004, *47*, 766–790.

Cameron, Kim S., and Ettington, Deborah R. "The Conceptual Foundations of Organizational Culture." In John C. Smart (ed.), *Higher Education: Handbook of Theory and Research*, Vol. 4. Norwell, Mass.: Kluwer, 1988.

Cameron, Kim S., and Freeman, Sarah J. "Cultural Congruence, Strength, and Type: Relationships to Effectiveness." *Research in Organizational Change and Development*, 1991, *5*, 23–58.

Cameron, Kim S., Freeman, Sarah J., and Mishra, Aneil K. "Best Practices in White-Collar Downsizing: Managing Contradictions." *Academy of Management Executive*, 1991, *5*, 57–73.

Cameron, Kim S., Freeman, Sarah J., and Mishra, Aneil K. "Downsizing and Redesigning Organizations." In George P. Huber and William H. Glick (eds.), *Organizational Change and Redesign*. New York: Oxford University Press, 1993.

Campbell, Donald T., and Fisk, D. W. "Convergent and Discriminant Validation by the Multitrait-Multimethod Matrix." *Psychological Bulletin*, 1959, *56*, 81–105.

Campbell, John P., Brownas, Edward A., Peterson, N. G., and Dunnette, Marvin D. *The Measurement of Organizational Effectiveness: A Review of Relevant Research and Opinion*. Minneapolis: Navy Personnel Research and Development Center, Personnel Decisions, 1974.

Childress, John R., and Senn, Larry E. *In the Eye of the Storm*. Los Angeles: Leadership Press, 1995.

Collett, Lee, and Mora, Carlos. "MOM Data Analysis." Working paper, University of Michigan School of Education and Executive Education Center, 1996.

Cox, Taylor. "The Multicultural Organization." *Academy of Management Executive*, 1991, *5*, 34–47.

CSC Index. *State of Reengineering Report (North America and Europe)*. Cambridge, Mass.: CSC Index, 1994.

Deal, Terrence E., and Kennedy, A. A. *Corporate Cultures: The Rights and Rituals of Corporate Life*. Boston: Addison-Wesley, 1982.

Deal, Terrence E., and Kennedy, A. A. "Culture: A New Look Through Old Lenses." *Journal of Applied Behavioral Sciences*, 1983, *19*, 498–506.

Denison, Daniel R. *Corporate Culture and Organizational Effectiveness*. Hoboken, N.J.: Wiley, 1990.

Denison, Daniel, Hooijberg, Robert, and Quinn, Robert E. "Paradox and Performance: Toward a Theory of Behavioral Complexity in Managerial Leadership." *Organizational Science*, 1995, 6, 524–540.

Enriquez, Juan. *As the Future Catches You*. New York: Crown Books, 2000.

Ernst, R. C. "Corporate Cultures and Effective Planning: An Introduction to the Organization Culture Grid." *Personnel Administrator*, 1985, 30, 49–60.

Fitzgerald, Thomas. "Can Change in Organizational Culture Really Be Managed?" *Organizational Dynamics*, 1988, 17, 4–16.

Frost, Peter, and Morgan, Gareth. "Symbols and Sensemaking: The Realization of a Framework." In Louis R. Pondy (ed.), *Organizational Symbolism*. Greenwich, Conn.: JAI Press, 1983.

Frost, Peter J., and others. *Reframing Organizational Culture*. Thousand Oaks, Calif.: Sage, 1991.

Geertz, Clifford. *The Interpretation of Cultures*. New York: Basic Books, 1983.

Gordon, G. G. (1985) "The Relationship Between Corporate Culture and Industry Sector and Corporate Performance." In Ralph H. Kilmann and Associates, *Gaining Control of the Corporate Culture*. San Francisco: Jossey-Bass, 1985.

Gordon, George W. "Industry Determinants of Organizational Culture." *Academy of Management Review*, 1991, 16, 396–415.

Gross, Tracy, Pascale, Richard, and Athos, Anthony. "The Reinvention Roller Coaster: Risking the Present for a Powerful Future." *Harvard Business Review*, November-December 1993, pp. 97–107.

Hampton-Turner, Charles. *Maps of the Mind*. Old Tappan, N.J.: Macmillan, 1981.

Hofstede, Geert. *Culture's Consequences*. Thousand Oaks, Calif.: Sage, 1980.

Hooijberg, Robert, and Petrock, Frank. "On Cultural Change: Using the Competing Values Framework to Help Leaders to a Transformational Strategy." *Human Resource Management*, 1993, 32, 29–51.

Jerimier, John M., Slocum, John W., Fry, Louis W., and Gaines, Jeannie. "Organizational Subcultures in a Soft Bureaucracy: Resistance Behind the Myth and Facade of an Official Culture." *Organization Science*, 1991, 2, 170–195.

Jung, Carl G. *Psychological Types*. London: Routledge, 1923.

Kets de Vries, M.F.R., and Miller, Danny. "Personality, Culture, and Organization." *Academy of Management Review*, 1986, 11, 266–279.

Kotter, John P., and Heskett, James L. *Corporate Culture and Performance*. New York: Free Press, 1992.

Kozlowski, Steve W. J., Chao, Georgia T., Smith, Eleanor M., and Hedlund, Jennifer. "Organizational Downsizing: Strategies, Interventions, and Research Implications." *International Review of Industrial and Organizational Psychology*, 1993, 8, 263–332.

Kruskal, Joseph B., and Wish, Myron. *Multidimensional Scaling*. Thousand Oaks, Calif.: Sage, 1978.

Likert, Rensis. *The Human Organization*. Old Tappan, N.J.: Macmillan, 1970.

Lincoln, James R. *Culture, Control, and Commitment: A Study of Work Organization and Work Attitudes in the United States and Japan*. New York: Percheron Press, 2003.

Lincoln, James R., Hanada, Mitsuyo, and Olson, Jon. "Cultural Orientations and Individual Reactions to Organizations." *Administrative Science Quarterly*, 1981, 26, 93–115.

Martin, Joanne. "Deconstructing Organizational Taboos: The Suppression of Gender Conflict in Organizations." *Organizational Science*, 1990, 1, 339–359.

Martin, Joanne. *Cultures in Organizations*. New York: Oxford University Press, 1992.

Martin, Joanne, Feldman, Martha, Hatch, Mary Jo, and Sitkin, Sim. "The Uniqueness Paradox in Organizational Stories." *Administrative Science Quarterly*, 1983, 28, 438–452.

Martin, Joanne, and Powers, Melanie. "Truth or Propaganda: The Value of a Good War Story." In Louis R. Pondy (ed.), *Organizational Symbolism*. Greenwich, Conn.: JAI Press, 1983.

Mason, Robert O., and Mitroff, Ian I. "A Program of Research in Management." *Management Science*, 1973, 19, 475–487.

McGregor, Douglas. *The Human Side of Enterprise*. New York: McGraw-Hill, 1960.

McKenney, James L., and Keen, Peter G. W. "How Managers' Minds Work." *Harvard Business Review*, May-June 1974, pp. 79–90.

Mitroff, Ian I. *Stakeholders of the Organizational Mind*. San Francisco: Jossey-Bass, 1983.

Mitroff, Ian I., and Kilmann, Ralph H. "Stories Managers Tell: A New Tool for Organizational Problem Solving." *Management Review*, 1975, 64, 18–28.

Mitroff, Ian I., and Kilmann, Ralph H. *Methodological Approaches to Social Science: Integrating Divergent Concepts and Theories*. San Francisco: Jossey-Bass, 1978.

Myers, Isabel B. and Briggs, Katherine C. *The Myers-Briggs Type Indicator*. Princeton, N.J.: Educational Testing Service, 1962.

Nadler, David A., and Tushman, Michael L. "A Congruence Model for Organizational Assessment." In Lawler, Edward E., III, Nadler, David A., and Cammann, Cortland (eds.), *Organizational Assessment: Perspectives on the Measurement of Organizational Behavior and the Quality of Working Life*. Hoboken, N.J.: Wiley, 1980.

O'Reilly, Charles. "Corporations, Culture, and Organizational Culture: Lessons from Silicon Valley Firms." Paper presented at the annual meeting of the Academy of Management, Dallas, Texas, August 1983.

O'Reilly, Charles, Chatman, Jennifer, and Caldwell, David. "People and Organizational Culture: A Profile Comparison Approach to Assessing

Person-Organization Fit." *Academy of Management Journal*, 1991, *34*, 487–516.

Ott, J. Steven. *The Organizational Culture Perspective*. Chicago: Dorsey Press, 1989.

Ouchi, William G. *Theory Z: How American Business Can Meet the Japanese Challenge*. Boston: Addison-Wesley, 1981.

Ouchi, William G., and Johnson, J. "Types of Organizational Control and Their Relationship to Emotional Well-Being." *Administrative Science Quarterly*, 1978, *23*, 293–317.

Pascale, Richard, and Athos, Anthony. *The Art of Japanese Management*. New York: Simon & Schuster, 1981.

Patton, George S. "The Famous Patton Speech, June 5, 1944, Somewhere in England." Recorded by Charles M. Province, George S. Patton Historical Society [http://www.pattonhq.com].

Peters, Tom J., and Waterman, Robert H. *In Search of Excellence*. New York: HarperCollins, 1982.

Peterson, Marvin, Cameron, Kim S., Spencer, Melinda, and White, Theodore. *Assessing the Organizational and Administrative Context for Teaching and Learning*. Ann Arbor, Mich.: NCRIPTAL, 1991.

Pfeffer, Jeffrey. "Producing Sustainable Competitive Advantage Through the Effective Management of People." *Academy of Management Executive*, 1995, *9*, 55–72.

Piaget, Jean. *The Moral Development of the Child*. New York: Harcourt Brace, 1932.

Porter, Michael. *Competitive Strategy*. New York: Free Press, 1980.

Prahalad, C. K., and Hamel, Gary. "The Core Competency of the Corporation." *Harvard Business Review*, 1990, *68*, 79–93.

Quinn, Robert E. *Beyond Rational Management: Mastering the Paradoxes and Competing Demands of High Performance*. San Francisco: Jossey-Bass, 1988.

Quinn, Robert E. *Deep Change*. San Francisco: Jossey-Bass, 1996.

Quinn, Robert E. *Change the World*. San Francisco: Jossey-Bass, 2000.

Quinn, Robert E., and Cameron, Kim S. "Organizational Life Cycles and Shifting Criteria of Effectiveness." *Management Science*, 1983, *29*, 33–51.

Quinn, Robert E., and Cameron, Kim S. *Paradox and Transformation: Toward a Framework of Change in Organization and Management*. Cambridge, Mass.: Ballinger, 1988.

Quinn, Robert E., Faerman, Susan, Thompson, Michael, and McGrath, Michael. *Becoming a Master Manager: A Competency-Based Framework*. Hoboken, N.J.: Wiley, 1990.

Quinn, Robert E., and Rohrbaugh, John. "A Spatial Model of Effectiveness Criteria: Toward a Competing Values Approach to Organizational Analysis. *Management Science*, 1983, *29*, 363–377.

Quinn, Robert E., and Spreitzer, Gretchen M. "The Psychometrics of the Competing Values Culture Instrument and an Analysis of the Impact of

Organizational Culture on Quality of Life." In Richard W. Woodman and William A. Pasmore (eds.), *Research in Organizational Change and Development*, Vol. 5. Greenwich, Conn.: JAI Press, 1991.

Sathe, Vijay. "Implications of Corporate Culture: A Manager's Guide to Action." *Organizational Dynamics*, 1983, *12*, 4–23.

Schein, Edgar H. "Organizational Culture." *Organizational Dynamics*, 1983, *12*, 13–28.

Schein, Edgar H. "Coming to a New Awareness of Organizational Culture." *Sloan Management Review*, 1984, *25*, 3–16.

Schein, Edgar H. *Organizational Culture and Leadership*. San Francisco: Jossey-Bass, 1985.

Staw, Barry M., Sandelands, Lance, and Dutton, Jane. "Threat-Rigidity Effects in Organizational Behavior: A Multilevel Analysis." *Administrative Science Quarterly*, 1981, *26*, 501–524.

Trice, Harrison, and Beyer, Janice. *The Cultures of Work Organizations*. Upper Saddle River, N.J.: Prentice Hall, 1993.

Trompenaars, Fons. *Riding the Waves of Culture: Understanding Diversity in Global Business*. Burr Ridge, Ill.: Irwin, 1992.

Tukey, John W. *Exploratory Data Analysis*. Boston: Addison-Wesley, 1977.

Ulrich, David O., and Brockbank, Wayne. *The HR Value Proposition*. Boston: Harvard Business School Press, 2005.

Van Maanen, John. "Police Socialization: A Longitudinal Examination of Job Attitudes in an Urban Police Department." *Administrative Science Quarterly*, 1975, *20*, 207–228.

Van Maanen, John, and Barley, Steven. "Occupational Communities: Culture and Control in Organizations." *Research in Organizational Behavior*, 1984, *6*, 287–365.

Van Maanen, John, and Barley, Steven. "Cultural Organization: Fragments of a Theory." In Peter Frost and others (eds.), *Organizational Culture*. Thousand Oaks, Calif.: Sage, 1985.

Waterman, Robert H., Peters, Tom J., and Phillips, J. R. "Structure Is Not Organization." *Business Horizons*, June 1980, pp. 50–63.

Weber, Max. *The Theory of Social and Economic Reform*. New York: Free Press, 1947.

Weick, Karl E. "Small Wins: Redefining the Scale of Social Problems." *American Psychologist*, 1984, *39*, 40–49.

Whetten, David A., and Cameron, Kim S. *Developing Management Skills*. (6th ed.) Boston: Addison-Wesley, 2005.

Wilkins, Alan L. *Developing Corporate Character: How to Successfully Change an Organization Without Destroying It*. San Francisco: Jossey-Bass, 1989.

Williamson, Oliver. *Markets and Hierarchies, Analysis and Antitrust Implications: A Study in the Economics of Internal Organization*. New York: Free Press, 1975.

Yeung, Arthur K. O., Brockbank, J. Wayne, and Ulrich, David O. "Organizational Culture and Human Resources Practices: An Empirical Assessment." In Richard W. Woodman and William A. Pasmore (eds.), *Research in Organizational Change and Development*, Vol. 5. Greenwich, Conn.: JAI Press, 1991.

Zammuto, Raymond F., and Krakower, Jack Y. "Quantitative and Qualitative Studies of Organizational Culture." In Richard W. Woodman and William A. Pasmore (eds.), *Research in Organizational Change and Development*, Vol. 5. Greenwich, Conn.: JAI Press, 1991.

Index

A

Accountability, designing, 99

Acculturation, managing, 121, *123, 128*, 214–216

Action plans, formulating: group engaged in, example of, 112; implementation, 87, 101–104; strategic, 87, 97–101

Ad hoc, defined, 43

Adaptability and stability, organizational culture creating both, 144

Adhocracy culture: appearance of, frequency of, 153; and average culture profiles, *75, 76, 77–78*; and a European company culture profile, *133, 134*; explanation and illustration of, 43–45; and human resource management, *52, 53*; initiating culture change to a, 188–190; and interpreting the culture profile, 72; and management skills and competencies, *120, 121, 123, 124, 128*, 203–208; and mature organizations, *58, 59*; and "Means-Does Not Mean" analysis, 87, *88, 95, 108*; and organizational effectiveness, 49, 156; and organizational leadership, 46, 47, *127, 127*; and the organizational life cycle, 53, 54–56, 57; percentage of firms dominated by, 154; and plotting profiles for individual items on the OCAI, 68, *226*; and plotting the culture profile, 64, 65, 66, 67, 69, 70, 86, *93, 94, 107, 222, 223*; and

plotting the management skills profile, *224, 225*; and psychometric analyses of the MSAI, 167, 168, *169*; as a quadrant of values, *35, 36*; and reliability of the OCAI, 154, 155; and strategic action plan development, 98; strategies, decision processes, and structures characterizing, 157; and total quality management, *50, 51*; trends involving, 79, 80; and validity of the OCAI, 158–159

Aiken, M., 17

Albertsons, 152

Alienation coefficient, 158, *159*

Alpert, S., 18, 32

American Airlines, 152

Anheuser-Busch, 152

Anthropological foundation, 145, 146, 148

Apollo 13 space mission, 44

Apple Computer Company, 49, 54–57, 72

Archer Daniels Midland (ADM), 152

Archetypes, 33, 150–151

Argyris, C., 41, 113

Arnold, D. R., 32

Associates Rating Form, 122

Associates' ratings, 122, *123*, 124–125, 126, 128, *129–131*

Athos, A., 2, 16, 41

Attribute, culture as an, 145, 146

Average culture profile: for each item on the OCAI, 76; for organizations, 75; for various industry groups, 77–78, 78–79

B

Bacharach, S. B., 17

Balanced organizations, 57, 72–73

Bancorp, fast-growing, cultural profile of, 65, 69, *70*

Bankers Trust, 152

Banking industry, 57

Bargaining power, low levels of, for buyers and suppliers, 3

Barley, S., 18

Barriers to entry, high, for potential competitors, 2

Behavioral change, importance of, 117. *See also* Individual change

Behavioral Data Services, 171

Beyer, J., 5, 19, 31, 145

Blauner, R., 17

Boeing, 34

Briggs, K. C., 33

Bright, D., 11

Brockbank, W., 51, 154, 161

Bureaucracy, classical attributes of, 37. *See also* Hierarchy culture

Burr, D., 42

Business organizations, study of organizational culture in, 154

Business Week, 117

Buyer bargaining power, levels of, 3

C

Caldwell, B., 2

Caldwell, D., 18

Cameron, K. S., 1, 5, 9, 10, 11, 19, 31, 33, 44, 47, 50, 53, 80, 119, 145, 147, 149, 150, 152, 155, 156, 160